D1625018

PRAISE FOR
GRAB THE HELM

"The sea of leadership books continues to expand. How Robert has chosen the helm of a sailboat as a metaphor is appropriate for our times, and nicely articulated. On the following pages, you will find ample topics and stories to stimulate self-learning about your leadership."

— **Paul Batz,** *CEO and Founder, Good Leadership*

"This book is a must-read for businesses and organizations who strive to improve employee engagement while discovering the leader within. I highly recommend it!"

— **John Reynolds,** *CEO, OMNIview, Inc.*

"Robert's work on developing Leading from the Helm brought a systemic view of organizations and leadership together in helping organizations develop greater effectiveness. Now he has brought the same thinking to our personal journeys, where each spoke adds to our ownership, clarity and ability to live life in the most meaningful way. This is a very practical and outstanding approach to self-development which I have long encouraged through work on the use of self concept in all helping professions."

— **David W. Jamieson,** *PhD Retired Professor; Doctorate in Organizational Development and Change, University of St. Thomas; Editor-in-Chief,* OD Review

"I recognized that Dr. Robert Sicora was an exceptional thought leader with a deep understanding of organizational effectiveness when I first met him. Now I know he is also a great storyteller. If you read and apply the ideas in *Grab the Helm,* your life will be enriched over and over again."

— **Ron Price,** *Founder, President, and CEO, Price & Associates*

"Dr. Sicora's research-based and actionable models are leading indicators designed to help take action and ownership by the employees in an organization. I have seen these models work first-hand, and I recommend *Grab the Helm* to anyone serious about impacting employee engagement in their organization."

— **Alain L. Thiry**, *President and COO,*
Salient Global Technologies

"Dr. Sicora has a unique ability to translate theory to practice and make it come alive in the organization's bottom line and employee engagement results. *Grab the Helm* allows managers and leaders to take esoteric theory and, valuing the diversity and contributions of every employee, turn that theory into something that will drive your organization forward and delight your customers."

— **Timothy J. Houle,** *MPA, DPA, County Administrator,*
Crowing County

"*Grab the Helm* provides a comprehensive and memorable approach to both personal and professional effectiveness. The helm models allow an individual or team to easily identify the specific spoke(s) most relevant to their current needs, while never losing sight of the broader, integrated system. It creates actionable focus in the midst of complexity and chaos!"

— **Val Schumacher,** *Head of Human Resources, Nexus*
Solutions

"Dr. Robert Sicora's expert facilitation and explanation of his leadership concepts increased the effectiveness of our already high-functioning team. His insights are transforming our team into purpose-driven leaders and improving communication and collaboration across all areas of our organization."

— **Aaron Graham,** *Senior Vice President of Sales and*
Marketing, Highland Homes

"Everyone can find something to take away from this book. *Grab the Helm* provides useful insights that can be used and practiced at any stage of life or in any phase of business."

— **Rick Bowers,** *President, TTI Success Insights*

"New author Dr. Robert Sicora is about to revolutionize the way we think about the intersection of leadership, engagement, and creating a culture of trust with his debut book, *Grab the Helm*. This is your playbook for building trust in your organization, setting sail on employee engagement, and facing the winds of change with your keel stabilized in purpose. This is not a book to be placed on a shelf. It is a practical guide with practical instructions on how to get your hands on the helm and steer toward success."

— **Charles F. Montreuil,** *Senior Vice President, Human Resources, Best Buy*

"*Grab the Helm* will help maximize your potential in life and leadership. Dr. Robert Sicora does a masterful job of reminding us that when we align with our purpose, we become purposeful in all that we do!"

— **Robb Holman,** *International Speaker and Bestselling Author*

"We've had the privilege of working directly with Dr. Sicora and know that this book and the real-life stories herein are in total integrity with his powerful message of navigating your purpose in the white waters of these disruptive times."

— **Craig and Patricia Neal,** *Co-Founders, Center for Purposeful Leadership*

"The core concepts taught within *Grab the Helm* will help us navigate, change, and improve student engagement within our program. Armed with an understanding of the eight spokes, our team can develop a stronger culture and improve our individual and collective impact."

— **Scott Tordeur,** *Student Compass Program Coordinator*

amplifypublishing.com

Grab the Helm: Navigating with Purpose: Charting a Course Through Life's Journey

For more information, please contact:
Amplify Publishing
620 Herndon Parkway #320
Herndon, VA 20170
info@amplifypublishing.com

CPSIA Code: PRV0121A
Library of Congress Control Number: 2020917701
ISBN-13: 978-1-64543-796-3

Printed in the United States of America

To the three Thomases:

Michael Thomas

Thomas Martin

&

Papa Thomas

GRAB THE HELM

Navigating with Purpose

Charting a Course Through Life's Journey

DR. ROBERT T. SICORA

TABLE OF
CONTENTS

REGISTER FOR
YOUR JOURNEY

This book provides a series of wonderful reflections and activities at the end of each chapter. There is also a workbook that complements the book and provides additional resources, as well as an entire website dedicated to you, the reader. This website allows you to access a library of resources beyond these pages and enables you to take electronic assessments and surveys that take you further on your journey.

Simply go to

grabthehelm.com

and register to begin your journey!

FOREWORD

CHARLES F. MONTREUIL
Senior Vice President, Human Resources
Best Buy

When I think of sailing, I first think of my Scandinavian heritage, as well as the ships and seafaring ways of the Vikings. Without the infamous low-draft sailing ships, the Viking expansion would never have been possible. Though the Viking ships were widely influential at the time, they had no helm, no centralized steering post. As such, the Viking seafarer was desperately vulnerable to being blown off course or shipwrecked in bad weather. Sometimes, the storm-weathered mariner would find his way home to tell of a sighting of a new land, but many more were lost without a trace.

This historical lesson—the importance of the helm, and how to use it to your advantage—is one that Dr. Robert Sicora has pinpointed in the research and practices he has honed throughout his career. I first met Robert in 1999 at Carlson

Companies, where we began to pioneer now commonplace human resource practices such as:

- Using employee surveys to gauge employee engagement.

- Linking employee engagement to company financial success.

- Applying Lean Six Sigma thinking to re-engineer HR processes prior to the implementation of human resource management systems.

More important, we developed a lifelong friendship, and through the years I watched him guide his young son as he navigated a stellar high school and collegiate tennis career. Throughout the years, we have shared our passion for hockey with both of our families (and have witnessed an NCAA national championship, but are still waiting for an elusive Stanley Cup).

In the late 2000s, I moved on to my current role with Best Buy, and Robert, soon after earning his doctorate in organization development, began to apply the principles we had learned together with his own new and emerging research-based thought leadership.

Early in my career at Best Buy, I enlisted Robert's assistance in helping my team understand my leadership tendencies and communication style. Robert forced me to become an observer as he laid out these results to the team. Watching the heads nod up and down at his conclusions made me realize that I had not developed the culture of trust that I needed to make this team successful. It was a turning point in my career, and I have never looked back.

Time and time again we have brought Robert back as his thinking and his thought leadership has continued to evolve.

His development of the purposeful culture of trust and its relationship to engagement is, without a doubt, a game changer.

In Robert's introduction and throughout the book, you see his passion for sailing. It is so appropriate that this topic is interwoven throughout the book. In a fleeting moment of craziness several years ago, Robert help me pick out a sailboat and put it on our lake. This little sixteen-foot slice of heaven operates on basic principles that are easy to read and understand, but difficult to follow if you do not have someone to teach you. There is a fine line between navigating the waves and the wind safely from the helm, versus the fight to stay upright when you lose your balance.

This book includes the basic principles needed to achieve that balance, and to successfully keep yourself, a team, or an organization afloat. An accessible and practical guide, *Grab the Helm* includes exercises that help reinforce the changes you need to make to be more successful. There is no greater feeling in the world than being on a boat, harnessing the wind and, with due respect, reaching an equilibrium with nature. When you lead from the helm in your organization, you get that same great feeling of knowing that your expert knowledge helps your employees sail forward in their jobs, engaged and confident in facing the future.

So welcome to an innovative, creative, and impact-oriented book that will give you the power of purpose and help you at the individual, team, and organizational level. Get ready to cast off.

PREFACE

still can't believe I got on that boat. If you have ever been to New Brunswick in eastern Canada, you may recall the beautiful, warm saltwater beaches or the lighthouses that dot the shoreline. Maybe you enjoyed some of the world's best lobster. But in 2015, I wasn't in New Brunswick for butter-drizzled delicacies or a relaxing vacation. I was in the riverside city of Miramichi to help my late brother's best friend sail home.

Dave worked in the construction business on large-scale projects—houses, office buildings, multiuse complexes. When my older brother, Tom, started up his own fine home remodeling business, Dave directed many clients Tom's way. Dave built the homes, and when the clients wanted additions later on, Tom got the first call. These two friends were both very driven and shared an intensity for life. They had developed a powerful relationship in and out of work. When Dave asked me to be his first mate on the trip, I figured it was the least I could do to help out a friend who had given my brother so much before he died. Plus, it would be a great sailing experience for me, someone who was just learning what it really meant to be a sailor—a win-win.

Dave had purchased a thirty-one-foot Pacific Seacraft he named *The North Star*—a nice, heavy-hulled boat—in Annapolis, Maryland. He got the idea to sail it home to Duluth, Minnesota, by way of the Saint Lawrence seaway and the chain of Great Lakes. This was a huge undertaking—over two thousand miles—and was going to take three summers. In the summer of 2015, on the first leg of the journey, he left Annapolis, sailed up the East Coast of the United States to Canada's maritime islands and the Bay of Saint Lawrence, where I joined him in Miramichi on a gorgeous Sunday evening. We headed down to the small fishing community of Escuminac, where *The North Star* was docked, to start our journey.

Escuminac is infamous for the Escuminac disaster of 1959, considered the worst fishing-related disaster in New Brunswick history. The remnant of an Atlantic hurricane had hit the village on June 19 and lasted three days, wiping out boats and parts of the town and killing thirty-five people—mostly fishermen who had been out on the water fishing for salmon.

Perhaps it was an omen. We arrived on the anniversary of the disaster, and the good weather in Miramichi had not traveled with us to Escuminac. A summer storm was kicking up gale force winds, and we would not be allowed to leave the harbor for at least two days.

I was disappointed at the delay, but I wasn't going to risk my life, and New Brunswick was as nice a place as any to spend a few days. Dave, on the other hand, wanted to get moving. He had a tight schedule to get home to and was growing increasingly anxious with the delay.

Following orders, we stayed put Sunday night and then again Monday. By the time Tuesday rolled around, Dave had had enough and was ready to get on the water. Instead of relaxing our two days in port, Dave had been a whirlwind of frantic energy, peppering the harbormaster, Marcella, with question after question: When would the winds die down? When could we get on the water? At what wind speed would it be safe to leave? Dave didn't like to sit still. He had always been driven and goal oriented, and he was exploring any and every option for getting *The North Star* on the water.

Grateful for her wisdom, hospitality, and patience—and because I knew Dave hadn't finished with his questions—I invited Marcella to join us for dinner that Monday night. While Dave asked Marcella yet more questions over seafood and iced tea, I kept my eyes on the National Oceanic and Atmospheric Administration (NOAA) website on my phone. They do a great job of weather forecasting, and I was looking for good news to pass on to Dave.

At one point, in the middle of his questions to Marcella, I nudged his arm. "Dave," I said. "Looks like about midnight tonight the winds will die down to twenty to twenty-five knots."

Marcella said, "That's still a lot of wind."

"Okay," I said. "It'll still be windy, but—"

"But it's not thirty or forty," Dave said, grabbing the phone from me. "Looks like it's going to weaken for about nine hours." He looked up. "You want to leave at midnight?"

"In a pitch-black storm under sub-gale conditions?" Marcella interjected.

I hesitated, not answering Dave directly. "*Into* gale-force conditions..."

"I think you can do it," said an older gentleman two tables away. He spoke with a thick maritime accent, and his weathered, ruddy face suggested he had been on a boat or two himself.

"Sorry?" one of us said.

"I think you can do it," he said again. "The only thing is, once you go out, you can't come back. There's no way to get past the wall again. And," he said, pointing his finger at us, "while you're out there, every harbor is going to look like a safe place to put in, but don't be fooled—they will be the jaws of death. In these conditions, there are no safe harbors. They will tear you apart. You cannot possibly get to shore safely. You've got to keep going."

"The water temp is in the fifties," Marcella added. "If you fall in, you will die of hypothermia in minutes."

I took another look at the map and furrowed my brow. "Normally, we sail about forty to sixty nautical miles a day. We're going to have to do—"

"—a hundred and sixty, that's right," Dave said.

"I think you can do it," the man said again. "But once you leave, you can't change your mind."

That was enough for Dave. He gulped down a last spoonful of chowder. "Let's go!"

Marcella put her hands over her face.

We left the restaurant and climbed into Marcella's truck. Dave was over the moon, and though I should have been terrified, I was excited to get underway too. I cherished the memories of sailing at night with my brother, Tom, and since I had just completed my nighttime navigation course in Charleston, South Carolina, two weeks earlier, I was eager to show what I could do as navigator and first mate.

After a few seconds of silent driving, Marcella said, "You know who that was, right?"

"No, why would we?" Dave glanced up from the NOAA forecast.

"Theodore Williston."

"Who?" I asked.

Marcella sighed. "The Escuminac disaster? Williston was the twenty-one-year-old captain who sailed directly into the storm instead of going for safe harbor."

"What happened?" I asked, now in awe of the man.

"His entire crew survived. One of the few crews that made it." She shook her head. "But that doesn't mean—"

Dave straightened up and broke out in a huge smile. "That's *exactly* what it means—we're listening to the right man!"

Dave and I started to get the boat ready at about midnight after only three hours of sleep below. It was pitch black, rainy, and cold. Marcella had left hours before and given us one last warning for us to ignore.

As we started out on the water, we could feel the wind, but it wasn't too bad. *Maybe Williston was right*, I thought to myself. *Maybe we can do this*. As soon as we got past the breakwall, though, we were hit by massive ten- to sixteen-foot rollers, which rocked the vessel like mad. "We're going to die," I said aloud. I had never experienced anything like it before, and neither had Dave, it seemed, by the look on his face.

Maybe we could return to harbor despite what Williston had said. I looked over my shoulder, but I saw that Williston was right. There was no way to get through the wave-tossed opening without smashing up on the concrete.

"Put your strap on," I said to Dave. "I wouldn't be surprised if one of us goes in."

"More like *when* one of us goes in," he said, latching in.

We lurched forward, determined to grit it out. After we had been underway just a few minutes, the lights and gauges blinked, then shut off. The only visible light was the glow of the backup compass. We had lost electricity. I stood at the helm, peering into darkness, knuckles white, just trying to hold on. We got hit by another enormous wave. My eyes burned from the salt spray and rain.

"I'm going under," Dave said. "See if I can fix it. I don't know how we can sail like this, no power or navigation." He disappeared below. I looked out and still saw nothing.

After about forty-five minutes, Dave called up from the safety of the bottom of the boat, his flashlight waving about. He hadn't been able to get the electricity up. Exhausted and discouraged, he asked me to grab the helm. "I'll relieve you in a bit—I just have to shut my eyes for a few. Just remember to keep us as close to a thirty-degree heading as you can. That's the only way we'll get to Perce."

"I got this," I said with more confidence than I felt. Dave gave me a thumbs-up and disappeared again into the darkness.

For five and a half hours, I stood clenching the cold metal of the helm. It was terrifying. I couldn't see anything but the deep black we headed into. I couldn't hear anything but the roar of the wind. I couldn't feel anything because my face was numb from the needle spray of the waves, my hands from gripping the helm, and my feet from the cold and standing in one place for so long. The waves hurled us back and forth, the compass reading anywhere between 330 and 120 degrees— well off Dave's mark. At one point I saw a pinprick of light through a break in the clouds. I guessed it was a star, so I used it to track our course. But all too soon it disappeared into the clouds, and I peered into the abyss once again.

Around the fourth hour, I saw something in the sky that looked like the lights of a city. I knew there was no city ahead of us—we faced nothing but ocean. I'm not sure if fear or the universe was playing a trick on me, but I thought the bright, crackling light of many colors must be the aurora borealis—the northern lights. I didn't know you could see the northern lights in a storm—and maybe you can't. But whatever it was, the powerful lights ahead inspired me with the hope I needed. Through the wind and the rain and what I thought could be imminent death, I held on to the helm with what I hoped would not be a death grip and gave myself a moment to wonder, *How on earth did I get here?*

*

I grew up in small business. My father, Papa Tom, owned a printing company of fifty-five employees. My first jobs were there—cutting grass, helping in the warehouse, learning the industry. It was impressive to me, watching my dad. He was both the president and CEO of this company he had built, but even more inspiring was the way he managed people. He was nurturing and compassionate, providing a strong sense of family, but still inspired the best in his people. He was a man I wanted to model when I went into business.

I am one of eight siblings, and most of us worked with Dad before we went out on our own. I am sure we got our entrepreneurial spirit from him. My oldest brother, Dean, supervised the back of the printing shop. My sister Mary ran an independent civil engineering firm with her husband in Wisconsin. Diane and her husband, Jim, started a court reporting business in Hawaii. Rita was one of the first women to climb telephone poles for Ma Bell. She worked her way up to supervisor, then retired to become our brother's office manager. Lynn, the adventurer of the family, traveled all over the country, including Alaska, working in production for small businesses. Tom had his own fine home remodeling business, as I mentioned, and Wayne, my younger brother, is a civil engineer.

I grew up watching my parents and siblings navigate the waters of small businesses, especially in the downtimes. I grew up in the 1970s, a tough economic time. Remember stagflation—high inflation and high unemployment? Drivers lined up for miles to fill their cars with gasoline. We drank powdered milk mixed with water, cheating our taste buds into believing we were eating our cereal as normal. In the 1980s, the economy rebounded, and we saw the return of growth, vitality, and entrepreneurism.

Though my whole family worked in small business, I decided on a different path. I was the first of the eight kids to get a college degree and eventually went on to get a master's and doctorate. I worked for many of the big companies—Pfizer, Pillsbury, Cargill, Eaton, the Carlson companies—where I was exposed to different business models and countless other learning opportunities: the balanced scorecard, Lean Six Sigma, ROI analysis, Gallup Q12, and other performance metrics tools.

The early 2000s were years of great economic growth, and I enjoyed the benefits of corporate life. But in 2008, the housing market crashed and the recession started. I recalled the scarcity of the 1970s and saw the writing on the wall. The big companies would no longer be the safe bet they once were. Small companies were struggling, and I wanted to help. It was time to test the waters and go independent.

In fact, I had always planned to go independent after I learned enough from the big companies—it was my original passion. My goal was to synthesize and streamline the models I had learned in corporations and apply those models to organizations of any size. My initial forays were largely successful. I went independent in 2009 and worked with a range of companies from 2 to 250,000 employees.

In 2010, I started a doctorate at the University of St. Thomas in Minnesota. I increased my knowledge of systems theory, cultural transformation, and process facilitation, and I learned how to apply these models to help organizations and individuals. On this foundation, I built my own models to develop an employee-led culture of continuous engagement, trust, and performance in organizations of all sizes. But I wasn't set on exactly what to call the model or what image represented it best. We used terms such as balanced scorecard, service profit chain, and service value wheel, but these metaphors didn't quite capture what I was striving for.

Meanwhile, my brother Tom was diagnosed with cancer. I put part of my work on hold to spend more time with him. If Tom wasn't fixing houses, he was on his sailboat, so that's where we hung out most often.

I could be an irritating little brother when I sailed with Tom, squeezing him for life wisdom and sailing tips. I had a huge passion for sailing, but I was essentially a novice, and I was thirsty to learn. I also wanted to get to know him better in the time he had left. On his part, he was keener to help me sail than to have any profound life talks.

Tom was an efficient sailor. He didn't let wind go to waste, and he carried this efficiency into his business. Everything he did in sailing and business had value, impact, and forward motion. He knew how to keep the moving parts working in concert, to hold them in balance—traits of an experienced sailor and a good older brother.

One weekend Tom and I were sailing on Lake Pepin, a large lake on the Mississippi River that separates Minnesota from Wisconsin. Tom was showing me just how aggressive a sailor he could be. He loved to tweak rookies like me, and the boat was heeling more than it should have been on a brisk, windy day.

He saw me holding the side of the boat. "Seasick?" he called out.

"I don't get seasick." I pushed myself up from the rail.

"If you *do* start feeling seasick," he said, "go grab the helm and look out at the horizon. It'll calm you."

"I don't get seasick," I reminded him, but remembered one of his great lessons in sailing: the easiest place for someone to learn to sail is at the helm. The helm is safe and stationary, and it gives you a feel for the boat. Taking the helm also keeps a novice from getting in the way of the more advanced tasks.

"Hey, I have to adjust the sails. Grab the helm for me anyway," he commanded.

As my brother trimmed the sails, I took the helm and looked out at the horizon on this blustery day, and then it hit me—the perfect model for my work. The helm. The helm is how you steer the boat, but it's also the symbol of command. It's where you have control—if you are willing to take it. You are at the helm of your own ship, your own organization, your own time, your own business, your own life. What a powerful metaphor. "Look out at what's in front of you," Tom explained in his lessons. When you're sailing, you always have to have two eyes out, so to speak: one eye on the horizon and the direction you're headed, the other on the watch for the obstacles and challenges that may affect you in a more immediate way—changes in the wind, tides, currents, and so on. To get where you're going, you have to keep your eyes on the horizon and your hands firmly on the helm.

I literally held in my hand the model I had been seeking for twenty years.

After this insight, I don't remember much else from that day. I'm sure we worked the boat, felt the sun and wind on our faces, and enjoyed each other's company.

Once I returned to land, I was eager to map out the new model. I had so many ideas and needed to put them on paper.

I called the first iteration Leadership *at* the Helm. I ran with this model for a few years until one day when giving a session, I asked the group, "Who do you see at the helm?"

"The captain," one supervisor said.

"The leader of the organization," someone else added.

I thought for a moment. "What is it we're really trying to embrace with this concept?"

A young woman who had been avidly following the ebbs and flows of the workshop said, "Aren't we trying to embrace the image of ourselves at the helm?"

Aha, yes, that's what I was trying get across. As a result of that exchange, we changed the name of the program to what is today: Leading *from* the Helm. We all lead from the helm—our own helm. Who else would you want at your helm? We all have the opportunity to be at the helm of our own ship. But it's a responsibility as well. Perhaps the most important responsibility of our lives.

*

Tom passed away February 11, 2011—our mother's birthday. I had many great experiences sailing with Tom, and both to honor his memory and because I have a passion for sailing, I dedicated myself to becoming a better sailor. A friend recommended learning on smaller boats, so I reached out to Tom's daughters, Britta and Hannah, who had been accomplished sailors from young ages and who taught sailing on Lake Calhoun (now called Bde Maka Ska). In the summer of 2011, on Tuesdays and Thursdays, I biked to the lake to take adult courses while my nieces sailed next to me, teaching kids. Learning how to sail was a blast. I reveled in the joy of feeling like a little kid out on the water for the first time.

From then on, I was hooked even more strongly, and I worked my way up to larger boats. My brother-in-law Warren had a larger one he docked on Lake Pepin. One weekend, remembering the times I had spent on that lake with Tom, I asked Warren to borrow his boat. He agreed. I asked my niece Hannah and my son Michael to come with me. I knew Hannah was the more accomplished sailor, but I made a deal with her; I asked her not to instruct me unless I was going to hurt someone or mess up the boat. I wanted to see how far I had come. She only intervened two or three times the whole weekend.

This was the first time I had been on Lake Pepin since Tom's death, and it was bittersweet. I missed Tom and the times we had spent on the lake getting to know each other in his last days. But now I was there with the next generation, Hannah and Michael, and the hope they represented. These are two overlapping memories I will cherish forever.

*

It was Tom I thought of when I woke the morning after the storm somewhere off the coast of New Brunswick, thankful for the night sailing he and I had done together. I'm sure it helped me get through the night. Dave had relieved me just before sunrise. Though I wanted nothing more than to see the glory of the sun after a night like that, I had passed out in the bed below from sheer exhaustion. Dave let me rest two hours before waking me—not to let me know we had made it the rest of the way, as I had hoped, but to inform me that he wanted breakfast.

I could have pushed him overboard.

Instead, as first mate, I fixed us both a little something to eat, but it was more of a snack than a meal, given that we had no electricity.

We sailed another ten hours and finally arrived at the city of Perce around six. Incredibly, we were only a thousand feet off our original mark.

I couldn't believe we had made it through the night, but I was elated and relieved that we had. I'm sure there have been sailors who have survived worse, but that was as close to the edge as I wanted to get. I was grateful—and amazed—that I had been able to hold onto the helm for almost six hours under those rocky conditions. It was the only thing that kept me sane, holding on to that helm. I knew I couldn't let go. I pushed away thoughts of death, and I called on reserves of courage and character that until that night I wasn't sure I had. Being at the helm gave me a sense of control in a situation that was as out of control as I ever wanted to be. There were too many things I still wanted to do with my life to have given in.

When we docked, I gave thanks for the safe landing, and Dave and I shared one of the best meals of my life.

*

Sailing through that stormy night with Dave reinforced to me just how powerful a model for living a life of purpose Leading from the Helm is. This book is arriving at a time of great change, great adversity, and great opportunity for all of us. At the time of writing, we are undergoing a world pandemic as well as calls for socioeconomic and racial equality. Many things are likely to change irrevocably, including some we don't even know about yet—how we communicate, how we do business, how we live our lives.

But every obstacle is an opportunity, and today we have the opportunity to tap into that core of passion, purpose, and leadership that rests inside every one of us to live an astounding life. I hope *Grab the Helm* inspires you to grab the helm of your own life and gives you useful tools for doing so. My goal is to help you keep hold of that helm throughout a lifetime of heavy weather so that you can wake to the sunrise of a fulfilling and engaging life of intention and purpose.

INTRODUCTION

With our program Leading from the Helm, Sicora Consulting has aided many organizations in maximizing their potential. Now we have found a way to maximize the potential of individuals as well—your potential—by helping you discover your life's purpose and align all aspects of your life in achieving it. This book, *Grab the Helm*, will guide you on your journey.

Who is this book written for? It's written for all of us on a quest for a better life, for those who ask the big questions.

One of the biggest questions, of course, is "What is the meaning of life?" The answer to this question has been debated by every great thinker, from college sophomores on late-night pizza binges to the eminent philosophers of antiquity and self-help gurus hawking their wares on TV.

I'm no philosopher, let alone self-help guru—I prefer facilitator or consultant—but through Leading from the Helm, I've worked with thousands of people and hundreds of organizations in the last thirty years to help figure out how individuals can best work in organizations and how organizations can best serve individuals. I've learned much from these experiences, but one of the most significant insights is that in our everyday lives, most of us are fairly practical. Not that we don't want to embrace the big ideas like *meaning*, but that concepts like meaning might be *too* big to get hold of as we face our daily tasks. How does meaning get us through the day, the week, the month, the next year?

The most important question may be much simpler—not "What is the meaning of life?", because after all, we've come no closer to an answer in thousands of years—but "How should I live my life?" or even more simply, "What is my purpose?"

Now that's a practical question we can all seek to answer, and I guarantee, once we find our purpose, we'll find our calling. I've seen it in my work time and again. I have to caution you, however, that discovering purpose is not a one-time thing but a daily quest. Purpose is not a monolithic end goal we achieve by piloting the ship of life to a mythic promised land and living happily ever after. No, purpose is a deeply felt, overriding aspiration, a way of life, a mindset that launches us on this voyage to meaning—and the next voyage, and the next one after that. A life of purpose is a never-ending quest, a life of intention. It's not only what sets us on the voyage; it's the voyage itself.

To extend the nautical metaphor (on which the whole concept of Leading from the Helm rests), purpose puts you at the helm of your own life. You're the skipper and the navigator. You plan the voyage, chart your course, choose your speed, determine the ports of call, use the helm to steer the ship. Who else would you want at the helm of your own life? If you give up the helm, you give up control, you give up intention. You embark on someone else's journey. How many times have you felt this way? That somewhere along the way you got sidetracked from living the life *you* desperately want to live?

If you get nothing else from this book, then at least understand this: you must have the courage to grab the helm of your own life. How do you do that? By finding your purpose.

Do you know what your purpose is? It's okay if you don't. Insight comes at different times to different people. These are important questions, and they don't always have easy answers.

That's what this book is about: to help you discover or reaffirm your purpose. We all have passions that drive us, value to contribute to the world, and special talents that help us do so. These combined give us our purpose. Finding your purpose gives your life direction and structure. It helps prioritize the hundreds of tasks you do every day, the hundreds of decisions you make, big and small. Purpose gives you insight into who you are, what you value, and what you have to offer. Once you find your purpose, everything you do will directly or indirectly align with that purpose. *Grab the Helm* will help you develop the self-awareness and courage to pursue your purpose and maximize your potential, as well as have a positive impact on your inner circle and the world at large. Purpose leads to meaning.

How do you embark on this journey?

First, a little more background. In the preface, I told you how I came to the idea of Leading from the Helm by sailing with my brother Tom. On one outing, with the wind whipping through the sails and the boat bobbing in the swells, Tom told me to grab the helm and look to the horizon if I felt queasy. I never really get seasick, but I took the helm anyway. That's when the model for my life's work fell into place. Because I worked mostly with organizations at the time, I imagined each spoke on the helm as one of the critical attributes that, combined with all the others, determines an organization's success.

Based on over twenty-five years of work in human resources and organization development, I designed the original model of Leading from the Helm to take a holistic approach to maximizing employee potential and driving organizational performance. For the past ten years, Leading from the Helm has been transforming organizations across the world. My team and I use Leading from the Helm to evaluate the organization's strategies, culture, processes, and people so that the employees and leaders understand how they can use their innate strengths to increase the organization's overall effectiveness and improve its return on investment. The model for the organizational helm rests on eight spokes:

Strategy: The True North; the overall purpose of the organization and how the organization plans to accomplish it.

Leadership: The development and awareness of specific leadership and communication styles, how they build trust into the culture, and the effect on teamwork and productivity. Everyone has leadership within them.

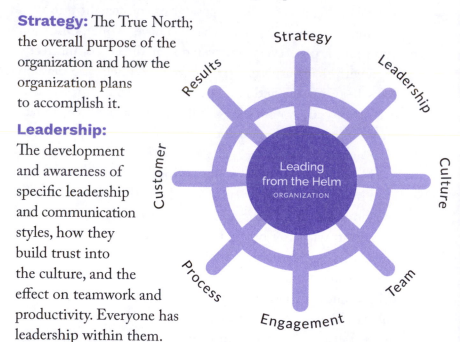

Culture: Organizational values and beliefs that align with strategy and personal values to foster an environment of trust.

Team: In an organization, the unit at which work gets done; for individuals, our inner circle, those we surround ourselves with and who inspire us to do better.

Engagement: Leveraging our talents, passions, and gifts to do the work of the organization with a positive attitude and enthusiasm. This is the leading-most indicator of performance.

Process: The services, programs, projects, and products produced for the customer. The systems and steps for how actual work gets done.

Customer: Whom we serve; how we contribute, both internally and externally.

Results: The contribution we make to the organization's goals, however they are measured. How we continue to create organizational impact and return on investment (ROI).

For organizations, Leading from the Helm aligns these elements in the pursuit of business objectives to ensure that employees, regardless of their title or function, are engaged and empowered to reach their full potential in the context of their work. We all have leadership qualities. When you look beyond titles and organizational structure, you see leaders at all levels, in all departments. Helping team members understand and leverage their innate strengths not only transforms their individual effectiveness and engagement but also increases the organization's bottom line.

In the course of our overall work with organizations, we also work directly with individual team members to help them make the organization more efficient and effective. But we learned something interesting in these workshops. Participants told us that not only did they feel as if they had become more effective at their jobs, but they also felt a renewed sense of purpose in their personal lives as well.

This was an aha moment for our program. If a tool like Leading from the Helm could change organizations for the better, why couldn't it make individual lives better as well?

That's how this book was born. We developed what we now call the Individual Helm by personalizing each of the eight spokes of the Organizational Helm in a way that connects the individual not just to the workplace but to any larger system, whether a civic organization, a sports team, a musical group, groups of faith, a club, a family, or even society at large.

While the two helms are distinct, each spoke is aligned with its counterpart on the other helm, providing a valuable framework for reintegrating and aligning personal values and goals into the larger entity. Setting aside the nautical metaphor for a moment, think of each person's helm with its eight spokes as one gear in a group of interlocking gears on one of those classic kids' games—you spin one gear and you move them all. *Grab the Helm* will give you the tools you need to move the one gear that spins all the other interlocking gears in your life.

The Individual Helm comprises eight spokes:

Purpose: How you live your life and why; what gives life meaning.

Self-Awareness: To know yourself. If you understand your personality and your communication and leadership styles, you can work through the obstacles that hold you back and become a better leader of yourself and others.

Values: Our principles and ethical and moral guidelines that help us make decisions; what we think is important.

Crew: Our inner circle, those we trust and surround ourselves with. We rely on them to both raise us up and challenge us, to give us feedback and support when we need it most.

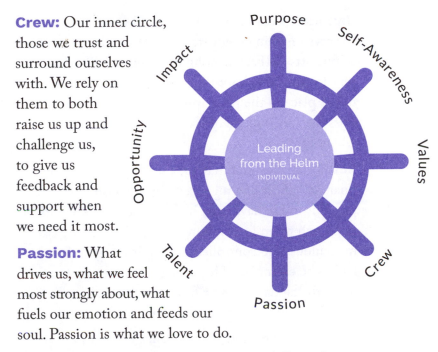

Passion: What drives us, what we feel most strongly about, what fuels our emotion and feeds our soul. Passion is what we love to do.

Talent: Our knowledge, gifts, abilities, skills, and even genius that give us the tools to act on each of the other spokes.

Opportunity: The chance, the opening, to act on our purpose, to follow our passions and all the other spokes of the helm. We can passively wait for our opportunities, or we can create them with intention. (Hint: It's better to create them with intention.)

Impact: The difference we make in our lives, the lives of others, and the world at large; our legacy. We have the greatest impact when we serve others.

To help you fully undertake *Grab the Helm's* transformational journey, we tell the stories of three main characters, Janelle, Louis, and Jim, as they (unknowingly) apply the spokes of the helm to their own life journeys.

- **Janelle:** A driven, reserved, late-blooming, twentysomething graduate student getting her masters of fine arts (MFA) in violin performance. She wants to play for the New York Philharmonic, but she's unsure of her place in the music program. She knows she'll miss the camaraderie of soccer, which she has played all her life.

- **Louis:** Janelle's grandfather, a seventy-year-old chief financial officer of a midsized organization. His two passions in life have been his career and family, with not much room for anything else. He's efficient, meticulous, and controlled, since he's always felt he's had to be exemplary. He expects everyone else to meet his high standards. As he faces retirement, he wonders what he might have missed and what's coming next.

- **Jim:** A middle-aged general manager for a car dealership who knows how to work hard, make money, and provide for his family. He's practical, competitive, and aggressive, and has doubts about the value of the MFA in music pursued by his daughter, Dionne (Janelle's roommate). He has sidelined his passion for woodworking to provide a more financially secure life for his family, but now he has an opportunity to help a friend on a house renovation project.

Given their different backgrounds, ages, interests, and so on, these characters confirm that it is never too late or too early to search for purpose in your life in an intentional way.

Each chapter discusses one of the spokes, tells part of the story, and provides exercises for reflection designed to help you absorb the lessons and apply them to your own life. When doing these exercises, take all the time you need. Be reflective and honest. But try not to overthink them. Focus on where you are today, and give yourself permission to use the exercises—and this book—in the way that is most helpful to *you*. Feel free to spend more time on the exercises that resonate—but don't avoid the ones that frighten you. Sometimes these are the most helpful of all.

The journey of self-discovery is continuous and ever rewarding. The goal of *Grab the Helm* is to aid you on this journey to living a life of intention by giving you the self-awareness and opportunities to do so; to celebrate your gifts and help you find the courage to live your purpose proudly; to reignite your passion; to solidify your values; to find the people in your life who raise you up; to make an impact.

In short, the main goal of this book is to put *you* at the helm of your own life and, in the process, lead you to your purpose and those all-too-elusive moments of meaning. *Grab the Helm* will take you on the journey of a lifetime—to align your purpose, values, passion, and talents and create an impact on the world around you.

CHAPTER 1

THE FIRST SPOKE
OF THE HELM
PURPOSE

If you have a pulse, you have a purpose.
—Richard Leider

Your purpose is what drives you, what gives life meaning. It is the "why" you do what you do. We touched on this in the introduction. Living a life of purpose is an innate desire, a need we all have to make sense of our lives, a calling. Our purpose connects us to the wider world. If we live our life in alignment with our inner longings and values and in appreciation of others living their lives the same way, we provide each other connection and stability in a time of change, chaos, and confusion.

Many of us, however, are living out of alignment. We haven't allowed ourselves the opportunity to explore our purpose or to align it with all the other aspects of our lives. Keep in mind that purpose isn't something you simply stumble on. You must cultivate it, create an intentional mindset in pursuit of it. What gets you up in the morning? What makes you excited for the day? In what moments do you feel most alive? Purpose isn't just a finite goal but a calling that you will discover with intention and awareness. Pay attention to what resonates with you, and then take hold of your helm and steer yourself in that direction. Leading from the Helm puts you in control of your own life. Take this opportunity to use the eight spokes of the helm to gain greater insight and clarity in finding and living your purpose.

JIM

Jim shifted in the driver's seat of his SUV. Driving his car was about the only time Jim sat still these days. Even as the general manager at Smith Toyota, he was rarely at his desk. He roamed the lot, looking for customers and sales reps to help out, customer service being his end all and be all. They called him the Bulldog—not because he was an attack dog, but because he never let go until everyone was happy.

But what about him? Was he happy? He wasn't even sure what that meant anymore. He was happy with his salary, that was certain, and his ability to provide for his family. But more and more these days, he wondered about the grind. He had started at the dealership in high school, washing cars and sweeping out the showroom. With nine kids in the family, his parents had no money to spare for college, so he joined the Navy, saved all he could, and when he mustered out, went to college for business. Meanwhile, to pay rent and buy groceries, he had gone back to the lot and worked his way up to a full sales position. By the time he graduated, though, he couldn't see being tied down at a desk, so he decided to stay on at the lot for a "little while." A little while turned into twenty-five years and there he still was, though his college degree had come in handy when he was promoted, first to sales manager, then to general manager.

He glanced to his right where his wife, Shauna, sat, content to watch the highway trees flash by. She was a good sport and a good partner. She understood his drive to succeed at the dealership and tolerated the working weekends and missed dinners with bemused laughter. He couldn't remember the last time all three of them—Jim, Shauna, and their daughter, Dionne—had sat down together. Did this car ride count? With their sales force down, the last month has been particularly busy for those who remained. But Shauna and Dionne had held him to his promise to take the day off to drive Dionne to graduate school, and here they were. Dionne was tucked in the back next to her green duffel, forgoing the view of trees for her phone.

The lot was a noisy and active place, and Jim wasn't used to the silence of the car ride. "You know, kiddo," he said, louder than he needed to in the close confines, "it's not too late."

Shauna turned toward her husband, *What now?* flashing on her face.

"Not too late for what, Dad?"

In the rearview, Jim saw Dionne had not taken her eyes off the phone. "Once we get you on campus, you could transfer to the business school, get your MBA."

"Yeah, because that's what all music MFAs do." She lifted her head, met Jim's gaze in the mirror. "This is one of the best music programs in the Midwest."

"I didn't say it isn't," Jim replied. "I just wonder what you're going to do afterward—you know, for life."

"Slow down, Bulldog," Shauna said.

"No, I want to know. What does she think she's going to do with a master's in music, no matter how prestigious?"

"I don't know, Dad. We've talked about this. Compose. Perform. Or teach. Perform *and* teach. Did you always know what you wanted to do?"

"I know what I didn't want to do. I didn't want to starve." He scratched his nose. "Actually, yeah, I knew what I wanted. I wanted a family. And once I got out of the Navy and met your mother"—he smiled and touched Shauna on the arm; she smiled back—"that's all that mattered. You do what it takes to provide for your family, and for me that meant staying at the dealership. It's been a good living. A real good living. You had it pretty good growing up, didn't you?"

"I know, Dad. I don't want you to think—"

"Did you know I almost quit the lot? My second year out of college, I was going to go into business with Patricia. You remember Pat?" He looked sideways at Shauna and in the mirror at Dionne.

Dionne fielded the question. "Yeah, with the construction company. How are she and her wife doing?"

"They're doing great. I just heard from her, in fact. Building homes all over the place. Anyway"—they didn't call him Bulldog for nothing—"I was going to be her finish carpenter. But your older brother came along, and it just didn't seem worth the risk. I always loved working with wood, though," he said wistfully.

"That explains the loft in my bedroom, the home theater, and the multilevel tree house in the backyard."

"Yeah, those were fun to build, weren't they?"

"Maybe if you had actually let me pound a nail," Dionne teased.

"For extra cash I used to do some work for Patricia on days off. This was before I was manager, of course. Which reminds me, honey." This time he looked at Shauna. "I have to tell you later what Pat asked me."

"What did she say?"

"Later. I don't want to lose my train of thought."

Shauna rolled her eyes.

"I'm going to let you in on a little secret, Dionne," Jim said, raising his finger in the air.

Dionne leaned forward, cupping her ear to listen.

"Okay. Here it is. I don't love selling cars."

Dionne and her mom laughed. "No way," they said in unison. "You're kidding."

"What?" he said. "I hate it when you gang up on me." He reloaded. "I don't love the work, but I love you. And your mom, and your brother. To support my family so that we live a good life—that's always been my purpose. And it's a good one. No pie in the sky singing 'Kumbaya.'"

Dionne snorted. "What does that even *mean*, Dad?"

"The point is, what's your goal? Do you even have one?"

"What kind of question is that?" Dionne blurted. "I don't know, Dad. My goal is to go to graduate school because I don't want to grow up and get a hard, boring job like yours, and once I'm there, to party every day until they kick me out."

"Funny."

"Seriously, Dad, I'm getting tired of this argument. I've always been good at piano. It's kind of been my life…you know, my passion. I owe it to myself to see how far I can take it. Don't you think? You're the one who paid for all the lessons. Whose idea was that?"

"Your mother's, actually. I thought it would be a nice little hobby, not a life choice."

"A nice little hobby?" Dionne said with real anger. "Is that what you think this is? I am not having this argument. Again." She picked up her phone and started swiping.

"She's not really mad?" Jim asked Shauna.

Shauna gave him her *What do you think?* look and turned back to the window.

"Honey?" he said, trying to catch Dionne's eye in the rearview. "Sweetheart?"

Dionne kept her eyes on the phone, and they continued on in silence.

LOUIS

Louis wasn't used to sitting around, either, at least not at their home, the nineteenth century Victorian he and Madeline had bought some twenty-five years before. As CFO of his firm, Khan & Penn, he did sit in his office a fair amount of the time, though, working through

spreadsheets, both the computer and hard-copy variety. He prided himself that he could use the company's accounting software as well as any of the young'uns, as he had come to call them.

After forty-five years at the firm, he still felt that as a onetime blue-collar kid in the C-suite, he had to be the best of the best and couldn't let down his guard for a second. He wasn't working just for himself and his family but for everyone who came after him. An old-fashioned sentiment, he knew, but at seventy years old and the first to get away from the family shop and go to college, he *was* old-fashioned, with old-fashioned values—intelligence, hard work, honesty, common sense. He was demanding of himself and others, and expected his team to meet his lofty standards. He knew this made some of his current colleagues see him as stiff and unapproachable, but he remembered the days when they were building out their systems. He and his team would put on an urn of coffee, take over the conference room, and pore through chains of code and stacks of spreadsheets to get exactly what they wanted. Now that had been fun, he remembered, and part of the fun was the give-and-take of smart and determined people working together to create something bigger than themselves.

Oddly, it was the success of the new systems that pulled him away from the people. He couldn't remember the last time he had gone out on the floor.

Louis sat on the wooden wraparound porch in a wicker armchair, reading a book. Trying to, anyway. It was Sunday, and with his wife, Madeline, at her sister's for the day, Louis wasn't sure what to do with himself. Fall was coming, the air crisper in the mornings and after the sun went down. The tips of the leaves on the oak tree that covered half the lawn were dipped in orange, and the acorns were dropping. He supposed he should get used to it, sitting around, given that he was retiring in a few weeks. He thought about heading into the basement to see if he could get started on the renovations Madeline wanted, but then remembered his skill with hand tools and thought he'd spare his wife the trip to the ER. He made a mental note to look for contractors the next day.

He closed the hardcover—a mystery Madeline had left on the porch—and placed it on the end table, a match to the chair he was sitting in. Maybe it was the colors in the leaves, maybe the approaching retirement, maybe the unscheduled solitude, but he was feeling more thoughtful than usual. He had two purposes in his life: his family and his career, "and not necessarily in that order," Madeline would tease. Louis knew that he was one of the lucky ones—that his passion had become his purpose. He had been teased as a boy for his excitement about math—until he shot up to his current six-foot-two-inches in the eighth grade. They left him alone after that, except to try to recruit him for the basketball team, which he successfully resisted. He was more of a cross-country guy.

"Forty-five years," Louis said out loud. In that forty-five years, he had helped take Khan & Penn from a three-person shop that had trouble meeting payroll to one hundred in the main office and another hundred in five satellite offices throughout the state. A good CFO was like the pilot of a ship, he liked to tell people. Instead of instruments, he used spreadsheets. To him, financial data wasn't cryptic mumbo jumbo, as so many of his colleagues seemed to think. It was the lifeblood of the company. He read data the way he imagined great writers read novels: with appreciation and attention to the different layers of meaning. That had been his purpose and his passion, so much so that a few years before, when the board offered him president and CEO, he had turned them down. As CEO he would have had to hand off the number crunching to someone else.

He always thought of himself as even-keeled, but he had to admit that the idea of retirement made him tense. What was he going to do when he grew up? Madeline suggested a hobby. What, take up golf at this age, or stamp collecting? Maybe he should reactivate his cross-country skills and run marathons. Did people actually do these things? He had never had time for anything like that before. He guessed he'd have to find a new purpose now.

This one had done well for his family, however—a nice house (admittedly in need of some repair), two boys through college, and now his oldest granddaughter starting her master's in music. Quite the legacy.

He'd allow that Madeline had had something to do with it, too. They had met in a college speech class where Madeline had won just about every debate and contest against him and everyone else in the class. He fell in love with her sharp intelligence combined with warmth and compassion, and they married once she finished law school, though he wasn't always sure what she saw in a gangly number cruncher like himself. She made partner after a long, hard-fought struggle during which she had to prove her worth every day, but she always seemed to have time for him and their two boys. Only recently had he come to realize how difficult that must have been. As hard as those days often were, though, he missed them now that they were past—kickball and tag in the summer, snowmen and hockey in the winter, 5:00 a.m. wakeup calls to dig out from a blizzard.

Madeline had retired from the law firm but seemed busier than ever these days, working part-time for Legal Aid and sitting on several boards. They had been together forty-five years, reared two good sons who were growing into two good men, and even had a couple of grandkids to spoil.

Grandkids! He glanced at his watch. He hadn't missed the call with his granddaughter Janelle, scheduled for a half hour from then. He retrieved the book from the table and took another crack at leisure.

JANELLE

Janelle unpacked the last of her bags in the bedroom of her grad school dormitory. She had decided to live on campus the first year of her music MFA, figuring it was closer to the music school and had fewer distractions than an off-campus apartment. She was hyperfocused and bent on avoiding distractions. She had come to violin later in life than most musicians—early in high school—and had worked hard to make up for lost time and skill. She was thrilled when she was accepted into this program— one of the best in the state, if not the country. She didn't want to mess it up.

She and her room- mate each had their own small bedroom, and they shared a common room. Everything was neat and organized, just as Janelle liked it. She had talked with Dionne, her roommate, a few weeks before—they were actually from the same city one state over—and Dionne didn't seem to care much about decorating, so Janelle had picked soft yellows and blues for the throw rugs and couch pillows to match the afghan her grandmother had crocheted for college. On the walls she had hung a few tasteful prints with musical themes, along with the hanging plant she had hauled from college to her apartment in the city and now to grad school. "My most loyal friend," she often joked.

In her own room, she hung pictures of friends and family, and her favorite inspirational poster: soccer star Alex Morgan of the U.S. Women's National Team saying: "Excuses are like losses. Everyone has them except the champions." She hoped to apply that intensity now to her music career. She had lain her college diploma on her desk to decide what to do with it. Framed in black, shiny-lettered with Latin and the deans' signatures, it showed that Midwest University had conferred upon her a bachelor of arts in music, summa cum laude. She admired it for a moment, remembering all the work that had gone into that degree—the aching shoulders, the calloused and bleeding fingers, the hours alone in the soundproof practice rooms—then put the diploma in her desk's file drawer. It was her dream to play in the New York Philharmonic, and if she was going to do that, she had to look forward, not backward.

Janelle had been on her own in the city for a couple years after college, so she had let her parents off the hook and moved herself in. Alone in the new room, on a new campus, in a new town, she was wondering if that had been such a great idea when she heard a muffled noise at the door and a rattling of the handle.

Janelle opened the door and saw a woman about her age with curly black hair and sharp green eyes peeking over the electronic piano she hugged awkwardly. Next to her, a huge green roller duffel had fallen onto its side, and the woman was about to trip over it.

"I got that," Janelle said, grabbing the bulky keyboard.

"Thanks." The woman shook out her arms, pulled the bag upright, and banged it into the room. Janelle winced, hoping there was nothing fragile in there. The other woman took a breath and looked around. "The place looks great. Janelle, I take it. I'm Dionne, by the way."

"Either that or you're in the wrong room. Nice to officially meet you." Janelle set down the keyboard on the couch, then moved in to shake Dionne's hand.

Dionne let go of the suitcase handle and pulled Janelle into a bear hug. "I'm a hugger," she said. "Better get used to it."

"I gathered," Janelle said, stepping out of the hug at her first opportunity.

The awkward lull of a first meeting rose between them.

"So-o-o," Janelle said. "I can't believe we're from the same city. Our high schools must've played each other. What sports did you play?"

"Yeah, I never did sports. Never saw the point." Now it was Dionne who had shut down the conversation, and each of them looked off into different corners of the room.

After several beats, Janelle finally said, "Do you need help with the rest of your stuff?"

"No, that's okay. My parents went over to admissions— something my dad wanted to straighten out, I don't know.

This is all I have for now." Dionne indicated the bag and keyboard. "My clothes and my baby."

Janelle laughed. "Mine's the violin. I never let it out of my sight."

With the tension broken, Dionne cleared the keyboard from the couch, Janelle produced two bottles of water from her bedroom fridge, and the two roommates sat and talked about music, awkward first days of school, and what they imagined the program would be like.

"Did you always want to be a musician?" Dionne asked at one point.

"Yeah, I think so. I mean, at least since high school. But who really knows what they want to do before that."

"That would be me," Dionne said, pointing at her chest with her thumb. "My mom put me in piano lessons when I was four. I guess I was a 'prodigy.'" She curled her fingers in air quotes. "It's all I really know."

"That's so…sad," Janelle laughed, hitting Dionne on the arm with a pillow.

"Says the lonely woman who hates to hug." Dionne grabbed the pillow next to her and swung it at Janelle's arm. She missed and the pillow soared across the room, nearly knocking down a new lamp. "Told you I didn't play sports." Dionne smiled sheepishly.

Janelle cracked up with laughter, and Dionne joined in. The awkwardness drained from the room.

When they stopped to catch their breaths, Dionne got serious again. "Yeah, I think I want a career in music, a nice long career. Composing, teaching, performing—I'm not picky. There's really nothing else that makes my heart so happy. Too bad my dad doesn't think so."

"Your dad doesn't approve?"

"Oh, he approves all right—as a *hobby*, he says. He wants me to get a real job."

"I'm sorry," Janelle said.

"I don't really want to talk about it. But hey, when they come back you can see for yourself. You want to go to dinner with us before they take off?"

Janelle pulled back into herself, fluffed the pillow, and returned it to its proper place by the arm of the sofa. "Please tell them thank you, but I just really want to make sure I'm prepared tomorrow. I thought I'd rehearse a bit."

"Rehearse what?" Dionne frowned. "It's the first day."

"It's just…I haven't played as long as some. Certainly not since I was four like you. I don't know. I don't want to give anyone a reason to think I shouldn't be here."

"Sure, no problem." Dionne looked down at her phone. "My parents are back. See you in a bit, I guess."

Janelle closed the door behind her new roommate. Was that rude? She hadn't meant to be, but she knew that sometimes her reticence was mistaken for rudeness. Grad school was a new beginning, right? She vowed to do better. From now on she'd be the new, outgoing Janelle. She laughed. Who was she kidding? The only time she had been even close to being that person was on the soccer field, where she had been varsity captain her senior year in high school and club captain in college. But now that she was set on the New York Philharmonic, she was done with soccer. She didn't want anything to distract her from her dream.

She retreated to her room, feeling a twinge of jealousy that Dionne's parents had gotten her into music so much earlier than Janelle's parents had. Why couldn't her own parents have done that?

Janelle flopped on her bed. And yet she was here. Studying for an MFA in violin performance. She knew what she wanted—something a lot of twenty-five-year-olds couldn't say, right? She had a purpose. She was going to be a violinist. She had studied hard in undergrad, surpassing all the kids who had been training since before they could talk. She had applied, auditioned, and gotten into one of the best music programs in the country. She had practiced all summer. She knew what she needed to do to get what she wanted.

So why did she feel so off, so out of place? Could you want something so bad you ruined it from the start?

To distract herself, Janelle took her violin from its case, careful not to scratch the burnished surface. She put on the shoulder rest, got out her sheet music, brought the bow up, and started to play the solo in Mozart's Concerto No. 5 in A Major. Ah, that was better.

Reflection and Activity

Our characters are not only at different stages in their lives, they are thinking about purpose in different ways. Janelle, the youngest of the three, is dead set on playing violin for the New York Philharmonic, a dream she is so committed to she is terrified she won't be good enough to achieve it. In the face of a looming midlife crisis, Jim is questioning his purpose. Is he going to be the general manager of a car dealership for the rest of his working life? On the other hand, Louis had found his purpose early in life and was lucky to be able to pursue it throughout his career. Now that he's retiring, what's next?

What about you? Do you know your purpose? It's okay if you don't. These activities in *Grab the Helm* are designed to help you explore.

Were you struck by any insights as you read the stories in this chapter? Did one in particular stand out? What comes to the surface for you?

Now, using a blank piece of paper, notebook, or journal, spend three to five minutes and answer this question: What is my purpose? There is no right or wrong answer. You are just starting on the journey. Write down anything that comes to mind in whatever form speaks to you—sentences, bullet points, words, images, finger painting.

Once you finish reflecting, determine a goal or series of goals that will help you achieve your purpose. Then ask yourself this question: What action can I take right now (today, tomorrow) to move toward that goal? For example, if you see your purpose as passing on wisdom to the next generation, what can you do today to take a step in that direction? You can research organizations like Boys & Girls Clubs in your area, for example. You can look into getting a teaching certificate. Pick something practical and relatively easy to accomplish.

A useful tool for breaking down purpose into manageable steps is what we call the 4G model:

- **Gifts**
- **Grow**
- **Give**
- **Gratitude**

The 4G model works like this: every day you choose to use your *gifts* to *grow* and *give* to others. You can use the 4G model to write these out in your journal. What are your gifts? How can you use them to grow personally? How can you use them to give to others, whether that be specific individuals like friends or family or larger groups? Finally, for the fourth G, write down your gratitudes of the day. Acknowledging your gratitudes puts you in a positive frame of mind, and a positive frame of mind makes it more likely you'll have the courage to strive to live your dreams.

I recommend doing this exercise at both the beginning and the end of the day (or at least one or the other to start). It encourages and reminds you of what you have accomplished and what you have going for you, and it opens you to opportunities for growth. In other words, it provides stepping stones toward finding your purpose.

Go to **www.grabthehelm.com** to enter your reflections and access more information.

CHAPTER 2

THE SECOND SPOKE
OF THE HELM
SELF-AWARENESS

*The privilege of a lifetime is
to become who you truly are.*

—Carl Jung

"Know thyself," said the ancient Greeks. This simple bit of wisdom is more valuable today than ever. If you understand yourself—if you are self-aware—you can understand others, and more importantly, you can understand how others see and interact with you. You can figure out what obstacles you are putting in your own way and become a better leader of yourself and a better partner or team member to others.

Self-awareness is at the core of emotional and social intelligence. Our ability to deal with change, to be resilient, and to effectively work through times of stress requires both an awareness of self and of the situation at hand. But we all have blind spots, and we aren't always aware of the impact we have on others. Our self-perceptions are clouded because, whether out of fear or ego, we resist reflection and feedback.

How do we gain self-awareness, then? We have to be open, and we have to be fearless. We have to have the discipline and fortitude to take time for intentional reflection, to ask for feedback, and to engage in facilitated introspection. Formal personality assessments like the one we describe at the end of this chapter are often a good place to begin.

Approaching self-awareness through these different lenses gives us a range of tools and skills to respond more effectively and empathetically in all situations but especially in situations that challenge us. This is critical to learning how to grab the helm. The more self-aware we are—the more we can be open to learning both our strengths and weaknesses—the more capable we'll be of facing great challenges with grace, dignity, and expertise.

JIM

"Where is she?" Jim grumbled, looking down at his phone. He and Shauna had parked in one of the visitor spots outside the dorm. "Did you text her?"

"I did," Shauna said, laying her phone on the console between the two seats. "It's been two minutes. She's probably talking to her roommate. You can afford to be a little more patient, you know. That poor admissions counselor."

"That poor admissions counselor should be better at her

job. I'm sorry, but when my daughter gets a scholarship and the numbers are jacked up, I expect an explanation."

"Which you received."

"After forty-five minutes."

"It was just a mix-up, Jim. And forty-five minutes is not that long to figure out something that complicated. Do you even know how you come off to people sometimes? Your aggressiveness? You scared that poor woman half to death. Not everyone operates that way." She laid her hand on his knee as if she could pass on her patience by touch.

"She should be used to it by now—she's in customer service, just like me. And her service left much to be desired. There's a reason I was the top Toyota sales rep for so many years and now I'm the general manager—customer service. You figure out what the customer needs, and you give it to them directly and completely, and you don't let go till you're done. It's about results, and you don't get results if you're a pushover. That 'poor admissions counselor' shouldn't have let me walk all over her. This world is tough, and you've got to fight for every inch." He turned in his seat to face Shauna.

"See what I mean, General Patton? If I didn't know you so well, you'd be scaring *me* right now." She put her hand on his shoulder. "You may be great at customer service, but you're not such a great customer." She picked up her phone and looked at the screen. "No response yet."

"What? I *am* a great customer. I know what I want, and I fight for it." He gripped the steering wheel with two hands like an IndyCar driver. Did his wife really think that about him?

"We all have blind spots, my love. As my grandmother used to say, 'You can catch more flies with honey than vinegar.' You should give it a try."

"But then you get all sticky and gooey, and who needs that? Be direct and cut to the chase, that's my motto." Jim's phone buzzed. "This better be Dionne. I don't want to get home at two in the morning." He looked at the number. "Actually, it's Patricia. Remember I told you she called me last week?"

Jim slid the icon to answer.

"Hi, Pat! I know I said I'd get back to you, but we're dropping Dionne off at graduate school."

"That's right," Pat said. "You told me that." Her voice was gruff from many years shouting orders on construction sites. "I don't want to interrupt, but do you have a minute?"

He checked with Shauna. She nodded.

"Sure, we're waiting on Dionne for dinner."

"Have you thought about that job I told you about? The basement remodel?"

"The basement job, yeah, I thought about it." Jim said it loud enough so Shauna could catch on and follow along.

"Well?"

"Things are a little tight at work right now. I don't know when I'd have the time. Can I think about it?" Jim scanned the parking lot while he focused on Pat's voice. Neatly trimmed trees offered shade without blocking all the sunlight, which filtered softly through the branches. Flat-topped hedges lined the walk to the front door. A pretty college—as if that mattered.

"That's why I'm calling. My client needs an answer. They've got some kind of party coming up. They need it done by then."

Shauna nudged him, then mouthed, "Why not?"

Jim turned away from Shauna. "That's really tempting, but if I have to answer right now, I have to say no.'"

"No? That's a shame. It's right up your alley—fine woodwork and some design too. More a restoration than a renovation. Fireplace, crown molding, custom staircase. We could use your expertise and customer service. If we do this job well, we'll probably get more work from this client. The house is one of those old Victorians that need a lot of repair. If you change your mind, I have to know soon."

"I won't. I can't. Sorry, Pat. Give Claire our best."

"I will. She misses you guys. Just think about it, all right? Gotta go. Bye."

He pressed the End button. "Pat needs some help on a job."

"And you said no? You always liked working with her. You haven't done that in a couple of years now."

"Yeah, since I became GM. But I know myself. I do like that work, more than the car lot these days, that's for sure. That's the problem. It'll distract me from my real job." He picked at the gray steering wheel cover with his thumbnail.

"You've got a ton of vacation coming, don't you? Take a couple of weeks. Have some fun."

"What if it's too much fun, and I never want to go back?"

"Would that be the worst thing?"

Would that be the worst thing? He couldn't say he hadn't thought about it. But no, he couldn't. He had responsibilities. You get to a certain point in your life and you have to be realistic. No more dreams. That's why Dionne and this music thing didn't make sense to him.

A knock on the window startled him. He unlocked the doors so Dionne could get in the back seat. "Hi, honey!"

Dionne got in the car without a word.

"Meet your new roommate? What's she like?"

Silence.

"How about the space? Plenty of room?"

More silence.

"We got the scholarship worked out."

Nothing.

"Still not talking to me?"

Dionne closed the door and picked up her phone.

"I'll take that as a yes. Darling?" He looked over at his wife with his you-deal-with-her face.

Shauna shrugged and said in a matter-of-fact tone, "I'm kind of on her side on this one."

LOUIS

His granddaughter had texted him to put off the call for another hour. Louis set the book aside. Clearly he wasn't ready for this kind of downtime. He looked around the yard. The landscape service took care of the mowing and the trimming and kept the weeds down, so there wasn't much to do. But the service came early in the week, and the acorns had spread out under the tree like a blanket of kids' marbles. What if someone fell and was injured? He could leave it to the service or—he could do it himself.

He gathered equipment from the old shed set back from the house: a leaf rake, the good stiff one to gather up the acorns; a flat shovel to pick them up; the wheelbarrow to haul them away; a pair of work gloves to protect his tender office hands from blisters. He chuckled at that. He'd sure come a long way from the family shop. He was glad his father had never held it against him—had in fact been proud of his son, the executive.

Louis divided the lawn into grids and raked the acorns into rows while the squirrels leapt from branch to branch in the tree, scolding him for stealing their food, he imagined. He got into a good rhythm and felt himself relax, though he certainly wasn't moving as fast as he had as a younger man.

This was the way he liked to work: by himself, with a well-planned job he knew he could accomplish. Sometimes other people just got in the way—it was like herding cats— but he was self-aware enough to know that as a leader in the firm, he had to work with his people. As CFO, though, he had found himself pulling away more and more, leaving the people stuff, as he jokingly called it, to his managers and team leads.

After all, his job was numbers, not people. Let the CEO and the HR folks handle that. Though he did remember the days before they expanded, when he was out on the floor, and how fast those days flew by. It was as if he hadn't even been working. Maybe he didn't like working alone as much as he thought. He just needed the right group. Some of the best times in his life had been those he spent with family—picnics, graduations, weekend game nights. He worked hard, but he always tried to make time for those closest to him. Maybe he wasn't the cold fish "they" seemed to think he was. He had a strong relationship with Madeline, of course, and he and Janelle got along well for the difference in their ages.

It wasn't that anyone disliked him at work—or that he disliked anyone himself. He was cordial on the way in the office and on the way out, but that was pretty much all people saw of him these days. He always did things by the book and was famous for his short meetings: present the facts, quick discussion, then get out. Everyone's time was valuable. To save even more time, he sometimes just sent a memo. His direct reports were so efficient and well trained that neither they nor their team members came into his office very often.

He did have friends in the office, though. Rebecca had worked with him for twenty years, and the CEO, Manuel, and he had coffee every Tuesday morning. But Louis guessed his reserve might have made him seem more distant to some of the newer employees, and the way that he ran things kept him out of sight for the most part. Louis didn't think good leaders had to be loud and commanding. His style was to lead by example and quiet confidence. Still, he wondered if he should have gotten out of his office more often these last few years.

Louis knew he wasn't a loner, not really. Nor was he shy—that was a common misunderstanding of people like him. People like him weren't any shier than the population as a whole. They were simply folks who needed time to process whatever they were thinking and feeling and, once they expended energy, needed downtime to recharge their batteries. Sometimes he envied the more outgoing people in his life, like Madeline, who could go from event to event and only seem to gain more energy and enthusiasm as she went. Today alone she had met up with her sister for church, after which they were going to have lunch, hit the outlet stores, and attend a dance recital of the child of someone they both worked with at Legal Aid—not even family. It exhausted him to think about. He could work long days when he had to, but he needed a good night's sleep to recover.

That was why he and Janelle got along so well. They bonded over their shared quietness, and Louis felt he could offer her tips on how to make her way in the land of the extroverts. Speaking of Janelle…he checked his watch. He had just enough time to rake this last row, clean up, and return everything to the shed before she called.

JANELLE

Janelle had just put down her string and bow when she heard the door open and people talking. Dionne and her family. Janelle quietly shut her slightly open door the rest of the way. It wasn't that she didn't want to meet her new roommate's parents, but it had been a long day, and she was sometimes overwhelmed when meeting new people. She was reserved like her grandfather. It exhausted her, and she didn't want to be tired on the first day of class.

Janelle thought she'd get ahead on the reading. Many artists were visual learners or enjoyed learning in more unorthodox ways. That was not Janelle. She always liked to be prepared and didn't understand people who could wing it. Even with a practical, artistic skill like music, she felt she understood more when she collected as much information as possible—that was how she learned best. Her grandfather had tried to explain it to her once. She was a thinker, an observer, he said. She needed plenty of time to work things through, and she grew anxious when she was put on the spot.

Over the years, she'd learned best doing things her way, and she usually did well on tests when she had time to study and in performances when she had time to rehearse. But she often received feedback from her teachers and professors that she needed to speak up more, to engage in the classroom. That was the frustrating part! People might not see it, but she was *always* engaged in the classroom, following the lectures and discussions, asking and answering questions in her head. Because it took her a while to take in information and mull it over, by the time she was ready to speak, though, the discussion had already gone on to something else. This frustrated her, made her anxious about graduate school. In college, she had been one of the better students in a small department, and her teachers had gotten to know her. But everyone here was smart and a great musician. Would they take the time to get to know her? Would they allow her to be herself? Would she fit in? She was afraid of being left behind in such a competitive environment.

To calm herself, Janelle put down her book—*Music Theory: Violin*—and made a list of to-dos for the next day:

- ☐ Wake up and rehearse for one hour
- ☐ Eat a healthy breakfast—smoothie?
- ☐ Leave for class early—learn the campus
- ☐ Sit in the front row
- ☐ Participate at least twice in class

Janelle looked over her list and immediately felt better. She was a planner and a prepper. Writing out her tasks and actions made them seem more possible. There they were in black and white, almost as if she could see into the future.

Laughter from the common room shook Janelle from her thoughts. Dionne didn't seem to think she was standoffish, at least not until she had turned down dinner. Now that she was hungry herself, Janelle wondered why she hadn't gone with them. Had she really accomplished that much in the hour or two they were gone? But she knew herself and didn't want to be off on the first day.

Maybe she should make it up to them and talk to them now. They were probably just unpacking. But if they were unpacking, maybe they wouldn't want to be interrupted. She should give them some family time. Or would they think she was rude? She didn't want them to think she was rude.

Sometimes Janelle just wanted to stop the merry-go-round in her brain, spinning in place and getting nowhere. From inertia rather than any conscious decision, she went back to her book, but found she couldn't concentrate. Here was her chance to show herself in a different light. She put her book down and added a box to her to-do list.

☐   Be more social

She checked the box, took a deep breath, and opened the door to her room.

Reflection and Activity

Just as they are at different phases in their quests for purpose, our main characters have varying degrees of self-awareness and different responses to what they learn about themselves.

Jim sees himself as a doer and a fighter. He's confident in these qualities, regards them as strengths, and doesn't always see how he comes across to others, including his own daughter.

Louis is a reserved thinker who understands how this side of him has influenced his life and brought him to this moment in time. He wonders if he should have done things differently at work, especially more recently—should he have delegated so much to his team and let himself become isolated?

Janelle is also a thinker. She understands what works best for her in a practical sense—that she learns by gathering information and giving herself time to analyze and synthesize it; that she's not shy but social interactions tire her out; that she needs downtime to recharge her batteries. But she is self-aware enough to realize that these same traits sometimes make her come off as aloof and closed off. She also constantly questions her actions and decisions, sometimes to the point of paralysis. She fears these aspects about her will hold her back in the music program so much that she actually puts an item on her to-do list: "Be more social."

Are you self-aware? Almost everyone answers yes to that question, but are any of us as self-aware as we think we are? Diagnostic models like the Four Colors of Insights and the Big Five personality traits are used by many personality-assessment tools, such as MBTI, DiSC, and Hogan. These tools help us understand who we are on a deeper level. They give you—and others who are using the tools along with you—insight into aspects of your styles that you sometimes can't see in yourself. They expose your blind spots. The self-awareness we acquire using these tools helps us adapt our style to communicate better with others, thereby building deeper trust. My team and I use these tools during every single Leading from the Helm workshop we conduct for our clients and individuals.

Four Color Energies

We are all a unique combination of traits, preferences, and behaviors. Personality assessments such as the Four Colors of

Insights give us a framework for developing self-awareness of our personalities. In this case, the framework is based on four colors (**Blue**, **Green**, Yellow, **Red**) that stand for different personality types, different energies. We have all four color energies within us, and it is the combination of these four colors that makes up the unique person we are. Once you understand your color energies, you can better understand how others see you and how you interact with them, and you can work together more effectively by developing a deeper sense of trust and appreciation.

We say that an individual *leads* with one of the colors. To determine the order of your four color energies, first ask yourself: Are you more reflective or expressive? If you are reflective, you often consider your thoughts and feelings before commenting aloud. Another term for this is introversion. In this case, you are likely to lead with either Blue or Green energy. If you find yourself leaning toward the other end of the continuum—the extroverted side of the model— you're more apt to think out loud, to share your thoughts more immediately. In this case, you likely lead with Red or Yellow energy.

How is it that you make your decisions? Are you more of a logical thinker? Or do you tend to be more relationship-focused and base your decision-making on how you feel? If it's the former, then you will lean toward Blue and Red energy. The latter leans toward Green and Yellow. To sum up:

Red energy = Expressive thinking

Yellow energy = Expressive feeling

Blue energy = Reflective thinking

Green energy = Reflective feeling

Thinking (Logic)

Blue	Red
Green	Yellow

Reflective (Introversion)

Expressive (Extroversion)

Feeling (Relationship)

Which quadrant do you lean toward? _____

All we are doing here is determining your leading color energy. So how do you figure out your second, third, and fourth colors?

By going deeper into the attributes of each of the four color energies. Read through the terms in the boxes on the chart on the next page, and choose all of the words you think best describe you. Be sure to pick at least one word from each box. Then list the four color energies in order from Most to Least associated with the words you chose. There are no right or wrong answers. In fact, on different days, in different circumstances, and in different situations, we may find the order of our color energies shifting. We call this adaptive behavior.

Thinking (Logic)

Precise Accurate Structured Analytical Logical	Assertive Competitive Driving Decisive Quick
Caring Patient Accommodating Sensitive Harmonious	Enthusiastic Sociable Active Inspiring Persuasive

Reflective (Introversion) — left

Expressive (Extroversion) — right

Feeling (Relationship)

1. _____ (Most)

2. _____

3. _____

4. _____ (Least)

Tip: *If you're struggling with this exercise, ask your partner or a good friend to go through it with you. Others often see things we don't.*

Here is a further breakdown of the four colors:

Blue energy: Introverted, reflective, thinking. Those who lead with Blue energy are apt to be task oriented, disciplined, careful, practical, structured, and objective. Attention, accuracy, and precision are their critical traits. They have a strong desire to understand. As a result, they are meticulous in gathering information and more efficient at processing this information internally.

Red energy: Extroverted, expressive, thinking. Those who lead with Red energy are more apt to be results driven, assertive, competitive, and headstrong. People with Red energy are often adventurous, persistent, and independent and like to keep things moving. They want to get things done by taking them into their own hands and are often looking ahead to the next objective.

Green energy: Introverted, reflective, feeling. Those who lead with Green energy tend to be more people focused, empathetic, and harmony seeking. Deep relationships are very important, as is developing trust. Those who lead with Green energy are usually loyal, caring, consistent, and sensitive to the needs of others. As a result, they are often very effective at consensus building and will go the extra mile to help others and build close relationships.

Yellow energy: Extroverted, expressive, feeling. Those who lead with Yellow energy are often imaginative, bright, optimistic, and socially adept. They have their eyes on the big picture. Cheerleaders and great motivators, they likely have a strong desire to connect with others, have a large network, and thrive on collective work. Those with Yellow energy create enthusiasm in both themselves and others, and enjoy expressing and receiving gratitude. They like to have fun!

You may notice that you identify with more than one color energy. This makes sense, because all of us have all four color energies within us. The assessment is not about labeling ourselves as one or the other but finding our preference and determining what color gives us our highest level of energy.

In fact, we tend to blend the energies in different ways at different times. For example, even though we may take a Blue sit-back-and-analyze-everything approach when facing new challenges, in situations we're familiar with—a sports team or book club we've been part of for years—we may adapt our Red or Yellow energy to be more expressive.

The colors are not meant to label or put you in a box but to give you insight into your preferred tendencies and how you may be perceived by others.

For example, I might describe Jim as someone who leads with Red energy—a driven extrovert who can connect with others. (He's in sales, after all.) But it is important to consider the top two energies. If Jim leads with Red but has Blue energy as his second color, he prefers just enough data to look at opportunities for improvement and then wants to drive for change—to get it done. This is unlike someone whose color energies are Red-Yellow. They are likely a big-picture thinker, an ideator, who prefers to motivate others to implement the ideas and doesn't want to drown in details. They want to talk about the possibilities for moving forward, to inspire others to achieve their goals. Both individuals lead with Red, but they have different personality styles based on their second color.

How would you categorize the other characters? What do you think their top two color energies are?

Jim:

1. Red

2. Blue

Janelle:

1. _____

2. _____

Louis:

1. _____

2. _____

Now that you're aware of your own four color energy mix, think about how you can adapt your style to help others feel more comfortable communicating and working with you. If you lead with strong Red energy (assertive, competitive) and are working with someone who leads with Green energy (caring, sensitive), your assertive nature may come across as aggressive and overwhelming or even combative. How can you use the four colors you recognize in both yourself and others to communicate more effectively and build trust?

Go to www.grabthehelm.com to enter your reflections and access more information.

CHAPTER 3

THE THIRD SPOKE
OF THE HELM
VALUES

*It's not hard to make decisions when
you know what your values are.*

—Roy Disney

Values are our guiding principles, the ethical and moral guidelines that help us make decisions. We derive our principles from the culture at large, the family we grew up in, and the individual beliefs we adopt throughout our lives. In this way, our values define who we are. They are at the core of the decisions we make and are the basis for building trust in our relationships. Values serve as a compass that points to what is most important to us and what it means to be true to ourselves.

When we consistently honor our values, we live authentically, with true purpose. We live with our whole being—we live with integrity. When we work against our values, whether out of fear or self-interest or laziness, life grows false. We become disconnected from our core. We lack integrity. We don't feel "right." And if we don't feel right about ourselves, then others won't feel right about us either. They will no longer give us their trust. The bonds of our relationships will fray.

In the previous chapter, we discussed the importance of self-awareness, of knowing who you are so you can make your way in the world and overcome the inevitable challenges. You must be self-aware about your values as well, and how you act on them—or don't act on them—in your life. Our values dictate our actions, and our actions show our true values—our true selves. Without self-awareness, we won't know our true values, and we won't be able to act on them.

Once you understand that your values are connected with all aspects of your life, you will be better able to align your values with your actions and live with integrity. And when you live with integrity, others are drawn to you. They find you trustworthy, they want to engage with you on a deeper personal level, they want to be inspired by you, they want to be led by you. This is an important element of Leading from the Helm.

JANELLE

Janelle instantly regretted her decision to join Dionne's family in the common room. What she had imagined as a friendly conversation appeared to be an argument, maybe the one about grad school Dionne had told her about earlier. This might not be the best way to meet the parents. Janelle put her imaginary blinders on and headed straight to the bathroom, hoping nobody would notice her. This was why she kept to herself most of the time.

She didn't really need to use the bathroom, so she turned on the cold water and splashed her face. That was more refreshing than she expected. She turned off the tap, and while she patted her face dry with the powder blue towel she had brought from home, she heard the voices grow even louder outside the door, especially the deep one she took to be the father's.

Janelle turned it over in her mind, what Dionne had told her about this ongoing family argument, and the more she thought about it, the more indignant she became for Dionne. Dionne was an adult, and in Janelle's family, her parents and grandparents had taught her to value everyone's opinion, and even if you didn't agree with them, their opinions deserved to be heard and respected. How else would you get to know what *their* principles were? Her family's values included speaking out in defense of those who needed support—her grandmother worked for Legal Aid. But given her reserved nature, Janelle sometimes struggled with putting this principle into practice.

As a twenty-five-year-old, some of Janelle's values had evolved over the years. She didn't go to church as often as she had as a child, she wasn't as much of a people pleaser, and she definitely didn't fuss for hours to get her hair just right. Though many of her principles had changed, loyalty and speaking out in defense of those who needed support had not. Remembering this gave her the jolt of courage to step out of the bathroom just in time to hear Dionne's father say, "Good thing I built that tree house in the backyard—because that's where you're going to live the rest of your life with a music degree."

The stocky, red-faced man in golf shorts and a blue polo was stalking the room as if he wasn't used to sitting down. His hair was business short rather than military, and he was graying at the temples and around the ears. As Janelle moved into the room, she saw that he was taller than he looked. A high school athlete, no doubt. The woman she assumed was the mom sat on the couch with the look of having been here before—not that she was giving in, but that she was used to picking her battles. Her hair was dyed a golden blond, and she had a warm, open face that now held a skeptical expression.

Dionne sat on the wooden coffee table, kicking at the edge of the rug beneath it, the hem of her tie-dyed skirt sliding up and down her shin, alternately revealing and covering purple socks. She had the look of a much younger girl being scolded.

Janelle's heart leapt for Dionne, then leapt for herself when the father stopped talking and the three of them turned toward her. Janelle gave a half wave, her hand at her waist. "Hi, um, everyone?" she said, sounding like a much younger girl herself. She was an adult! Why didn't she feel like one?

Dionne stood up, stepped toward Janelle, then stopped, turned back to her parents. "Mom, Dad. My new roomie."

"Janelle," Janelle announced, extending her arm for a handshake. When in doubt, fall back on manners, her parents and grandparents had taught her.

"Sorry if we disrupted you with our family, uh, discussion," Dionne's father said. "I'm Jim. Jim Riley." He covered the ground to Janelle in one long stride and took her in what was apparently the family bear hug. Meanwhile the mother stood up, waited her turn, then jumped in when the father backed away. "Call me Shauna."

"Nice to meet you both," Janelle said. With her eyes she pleaded to Dionne, *Help!*

Dionne laughed, returning to the outgoing, confident woman Janelle had met earlier that day. "All right, all right, break it up. She's not much of a hugger, this one." Then to Janelle she said, "I told you to get used to it."

"That's good advice," said Shauna. "Especially when you visit the house over break. You don't live far, I understand. Everyone's a hugger in our family."

Oh, no, Janelle thought. A whole family of live wires!

As if to prove her point, Jim put Janelle on the spot right away. "What does *your* family think about throwing away good money on this music stuff?"

"Jim," the mother said, batting him on the arm.

"Dad!" said Dionne.

But Jim didn't back down. He looked at Janelle intensely, though not unkindly, as if he was truly interested in her answer.

Janelle's first instinct was to dash back into her room, order a bolt lock online, and barricade herself until they all went away. But she had her principles, and speaking out was one of them. She collected her thoughts, took a deep breath, then spoke carefully, lining up her points as she went. "Getting into this program has been my life's dream—ever since I discovered the violin in high school, anyway. I know music is a risky field, but it's not the only one that's risky. We can perform, we can teach, we can compose, we can run a music store, become an artistic director. We can also change our minds later, but I won't, unless I'm really terrible. With the cost of education, many fields are a risk, but I'm happy with the investment I'm making in myself. Music takes discipline and hard work, and you can apply those traits to just about anything. Education is really important to me, and I think I made the right choice."

Dionne eyes widened in amazement.

Then Janelle got even bolder. "Let me ask you this, sir."

Jim nodded. He seemed to like the "sir."

"You look like you played some sports, right? I was on the soccer team."

"Football," he said, pulling back his shoulders. "Outside linebacker. Lettered three years."

"Okay. What do you do now?"

He cocked his head, as if to say *What's it to you?* But he answered directly. "General manager at a car dealership. It's a good living." He looked to Dionne and her mother for confirmation. They both nodded.

"I'm sure it is," Janelle said sincerely. "But no football. You didn't go pro, you don't coach now."

He shook his head.

"Why'd you do it, then? Why'd you play football?"

"It was fun."

"Okay."

"It was good exercise."

"Of course."

"We learned good teamwork and discipline." Jim broke out in a smile. "All right, young lady, you might have a point there. But we didn't have to pay tuition to play football, and I never planned to make it my life."

"But it did cost something, I'm sure, if not just a lot of time and effort. At least soccer did for me."

"Yeah, I guess it did. But it was worth it."

"Well, I think *this* is worth it." She spread out her arms to include the room and the whole campus.

"But I just—worry for you girls." Then he got a twinkle in his eye. "With arguments like that, though, you could go to law school." Then he turned to his daughter. "Honey, have *you* ever thought of law school? You argue with me all the time. You and Janelle could transfer and—"

"Give it up, already, will you, Dad? No wonder they call you Bulldog."

While she was feeling brave, Janelle went on. "I applied three times to get into this program. They only take the best of the best, and your daughter got in first try. Honestly, if anyone should be worried, it's *my* parents."

Shauna laughed. "None of us need to worry. Both of you girls will do just fine." She hugged Janelle. "We have to get on the road, James," she said to her husband, who stepped in to hug Dionne, a shadow of sadness crossing his face. Then Shauna hugged her daughter. "Don't forget to call. You call your family, don't you, Janelle?"

"Oh no," she said, glancing at the clock on the microwave. "I should have called an hour ago. Gotta go. Nice meeting you." Janelle dashed into her room to find her cell phone.

LOUIS

"I thought you had forgotten your old grandpa." Louis had put the equipment away and was drying his hands in the hall bathroom when the call came in. He walked to the den as he spoke.

"Never, Papa. I just got caught up with my roommate and her parents. We were discussing the value of an MFA in music."

"Ah," he said. "For or against?"

Janelle laughed. "You always get to the point, don't you? My roommate and me for, of course. Dionne's—that's my roommate's—dad against. I think her mom was just enjoying the show."

Louis groaned as he sat in his recliner. Perhaps he should have stretched before raking.

"That was a big groan," Janelle said. "You all right over there?"

"Just a little yard work."

"Maybe you should take it easy, now that you're retiring."

"Or get used to doing more." He rubbed the shoulder of the arm holding the phone. "Everything work out in your 'discussion'?"

"I think we talked the dad around a little. At least enough to get him to lay off Dionne for a while. He's one of these hard-nosed types. Thinks everything's an episode of *Survivor*. He loves Dionne, though, I can tell that. He got all sad when it was time to say good-bye. Very cute. Remember that stuff you told me about outgoing and analytic people?"

"Of course."

"Definitely an outgoing family. I'm exhausted and kind of jittery. Do you think I was out of line? I'm trying to put myself out there, but I don't want to be rude."

"I've always known you to be respectful in your discussions. You learned that from your grandma. Sweet as pie, but I don't think she's lost an argument in her life. A few cases, maybe, but not an argument."

"No one's ever called me sweet as pie, and as for the argument, I was lucky if I came out even."

"*I* think you're sweet as pie," Louis said.

"Thank you, Papa. But—"

"But I don't count?"

"I was going to say, but you're biased."

"I absolutely am biased. You know how much I value family. Family and work. That's been my life. Not much room for anything else."

"Me too, Papa, but I've got a question for you."

"Shoot."

"What if the work you do doesn't have that much value, at least in other people's eyes? People don't seem to value music much. I mean, would you value your work if you hadn't made so much money?"

"Oh, hon. No one should ever mistake you for shy. First off, I probably don't make as much money as you think. Remember, your grandma was a very good attorney. She made a fair amount herself. But I've done all right. Second, don't make the mistake of equating value with money. Sure, money comes in handy for the basics—food and shelter and other things we need to survive, as well as some of the niceties. But the kind of values we're talking about are intrinsic. They're more about the principles that guide your decisions. You value expressing yourself through music. You've aligned your life to make that happen. As long as you do it responsibly—without committing crimes, without expecting others to do it for you, without starving your children—then your values are as important as anyone's. And to answer your other question, yes, I think I would still do what I do even if I didn't make as much money. Number crunching is in my bones like music is in yours. What you value is what you value, and as long as you respect other people's principles, you certainly have the right to follow your own. And values evolve. I'm facing that a little myself right now with this retirement."

"How's that going? Besides the yard work."

"If today's any indication, I'm facing a huge learning curve." He sighed.

"Oh, Papa. You're going to be the best retired person ever. You wouldn't accept anything less."

"Yeah, but now that I won't have work to occupy my time, I don't actually know what I'm going to do. That's one half of my family/work equation gone in one fell swoop. I should have planned for this better."

"You just have to find something you value as much as work."

"Huh," he said, pausing thoughtfully. "I was thinking I needed to find something to *do*. But if I find something to *value*, the doing should take care of itself. You're a very wise young woman. I just have to figure out what that is."

"I learned from the best. And you'll find something, Papa. Then there will be no holding you back." Her tone became more serious. "I'm sorry I won't be able to make your office retirement party. School kind of came at a bad time for that."

"Oh, honey. School never comes at a bad time—I'm so happy you're there. You are right where you need to be, and at the exact right time."

"Thanks, Papa. I wish I was as sure about that as you are."

"Hey, hey. I know this may seem a little daunting, but you know what? They wanted you. If they didn't think you could do it, they wouldn't have let you in."

"I guess so."

"You know so. Just concentrate on what's important to you: planning, hard work, musicianship. One step at a time."

"You're right." Her voice seemed to perk up a bit. "That's all I can do. You too!"

"That's a deal," Louis said.

"See you at the family party."

"Only if you can make it. School comes first."

"You're a great mentor, Papa. Talk to you soon. Love you."

"Love you too."

Great mentor? Louis thought he was just being a great grandfather. Something else to think about in retirement.

JIM

Jim and Shauna were back on the road, just the two of them, the hum of the air conditioner bracketing their silence. *Don't tell me she's mad at me too,* Jim was thinking. He looked over at Shauna to make sure. The corners of her mouth were turned up in amusement rather than anger. Not mad, then. "What's so funny?" he said at a moderate volume for him.

"She got you, that roommate, Janelle. You have to watch out for the quiet ones."

"She wasn't that—"

"She got you, plain and simple. Just admit it."

"Yeah, she pretty much did."

They both laughed.

"You know I just want what's best for Dionne, right? We taught her solid values, and now she's—"

"Putting them into action?" Shauna interjected.

"What?" he said. "How do you figure?"

She counted off on her fingers. "The drive to succeed. Setting stretch goals. High energy. Self-reliance. Responsibility. These are all principles *we've* taught her."

"I guess, but—"

"No buts. She got her values from us. She's just applying them differently, making different decisions. Do you think she's being irresponsible?"

"No. Well, maybe a little."

"She wouldn't have joined the program if she hadn't received the fellowship. You know that, right?"

"No, she never said."

"She was going to do it on her own or not at all."

He hadn't thought about it that way, how the same values could take you down different paths. His daughter was investing in herself, just as he had when he joined the Navy. And she was a hard worker, he had to give her that. Piano since she was four. In junior high, he had lasted on the trombone for half a lesson.

"She's just trying to follow what's important to her," Shauna added.

"She certainly didn't learn that from me."

"You don't value selling cars?" She touched his knee.

"I value security for our family—for you and Dionne and David," he said, intertwining his fingers with hers.

"For which we are eternally grateful. Really, honey. Genuinely grateful. My teacher's salary couldn't have supported the family. But Dionne and David are on their own now, so maybe it's time."

"Time for what?"

"Time for anything. What do you want to be when you grow up?"

"That's no secret. You know I love working with my hands, working with wood. Designing things. Building things. But it doesn't really pay, you know, homemade furniture."

"I know. We've got more bookshelves in the garage than we know what to do with. I'm not talking about furniture. What about Pat's job?"

"The basement remodel?"

"You used to do that for her all the time."

"You heard. She needed an answer today, so I told her no. I just don't have the bandwidth right now."

"You have a ton of vacation coming—lord knows you never take time off. Why don't you take a few weeks and do the job? You owe it to yourself—and to us."

"To 'us'?"

"Us. Your family. You've done great by us, but now you owe it to us to do this. You've done your duty, now pursue your dream. You've been a little cranky lately."

"I have not."

She gave him a look.

"Okay, maybe a little. I do wonder sometimes if there's more than the dealership, you know? But I can't let myself think about that. It's too tempting."

"First of all, you think about it all the time, I can see it on your face, so you're not fooling anyone. And second, it's just for a few weeks, not the rest of your life."

"What about my team? What about the customers?"

"Don't let them go home until they're happy," Shauna intoned. Then she snorted.

"What?" Jim said.

"I just remembered something Dionne used to say when she was little and you stayed late with a customer."

"What's that?"

"Mommy, why can't we be Daddy's customer?"

"She did not!" He slapped the steering wheel.

"Oh, yes she did."

Had she really? If you saw it like that, that his daughter *was* one of his customers—and his wife and son too—then maybe he was not giving them the best of himself. He had always strived to be a great provider, and he knew he was. But he had to admit that sometimes he let that role define the way he looked at the world, and that he measured everything—and everyone—on that scale. Did it pay off? But did everything have to pay off, at least in a literal way? Didn't his family deserve to be as happy as his customers? Was he as true to his values as he thought? As true to himself?

He looked out at the next couple weeks. Usually the owner wanted more notice than this for time off, but Jim had known him for years, so that wouldn't be a problem. Marvin could step in as acting GM—he was gunning for it anyway.

"Do you think I should?" he said. "Take Pat's job?"

"I do. Then maybe you won't be so cranky—and you'll learn how Dionne feels about her music."

"Do you mind driving for a while if I pull over? I have to make a few phone calls."

"A new day for the Bulldog!" Shauna smacked him on the arm. "You're letting me drive *and* putting in for PTO."

"Watch what you ask for." He smiled as he pulled into the right lane to get off at the next exit. "I always wanted a limo driver."

Reflection and Activity

What do you observe about the values of the characters in the story? Do they act in alignment with their values? In other words, do they act with integrity?

What about your own values? What are they? What is it that you believe in? On what core principles do you base your decisions, especially your major ones?

This brief exercise will help you identify what you value.

Using your favorite tool for brainstorming—legal pad, journal, tablet, laptop, whiteboard, chalkboard, whatever it may be—spend three to five minutes writing down what you truly value. Don't think too much about it—respond from the heart. Common values include things like love, wisdom, self-reliance, strength, and so on. (If you have trouble coming up with specific terms, google "core values" and you'll find dozens of lists.) Your list can be as long as you want, and if you're on a roll, you don't have to stop at five minutes. Aim for at least ten to twelve items. Your list doesn't even have to be a list per se. Arrange the items any way that works for you—clouds, stars, circles, and so on.

It is very important to be honest. Don't write down what you think you *should* value—write down what you *do* value. If you value making as much money as possible, then write that down. If you value world peace, then write that down. If you value both, then write them both. It's your list.

If you're stuck, another activity you can do is to look at your credit card statements and calendar. Where do you spend your money? Do you like to shop online? Do you save up for travel? Do you attend sporting events frequently? Similarly, where do you spend most of your free time? A weekly faith group? Coaching your niece's softball team? Do you stay long hours at work?

When you finish brainstorming, put your writing tool aside for a moment, and reflect on what you wrote. Are there any surprises? Did you forget anything? (Add those now.) Do you see any common themes in your list? If you can identify some (family, education, integrity, money, and so on), group them into categories. The classification will help you visualize and narrow down what is important to you, especially if you have a lot of choices. After you review what you wrote, circle your top five values—those you consider the most central to your life, the most critical to your decision-making.

Then ask yourself this: Do you live those values?

Think about it deeply and honestly. Do you live your core values? For the next week, observe how your behavior—how your decisions and actions—aligns with those values or conflicts with them. Are you consistent? Are there areas of your life (work, extracurricular activities, friendships, relationships, and so on) in which your actions don't follow your principles?

If you notice a disconnect, work on self-awareness. Perhaps you truly do not value what you thought you did. It may be time to recalibrate. Or maybe what you truly value gets lost in everyday chaos. In that case, it's time to rededicate yourself to aligning your values with the way you live.

Go to www.grabthehelm.com to enter your reflections and access more information.

CHAPTER 4

THE FOURTH SPOKE OF THE HELM
CREW

Alone we can do so little;
together we can do so much.

—Helen Keller

All but the smallest boats don't get very far without a crew to operate them. A boat crew is an intricate, well-oiled machine that depends on a group of people with a range of talents working in harmony and trust toward a common goal—a purpose—in this case, to get from point A to point B on a large body of water. In a similar way, we all need a crew—a tight-knit group of trusted individuals—to help carry us through life. No matter how much we promote the myth of rugged individualism, the fact is that none of us can do much on our own, as the quotation from Helen Keller affirms. As part of a trusted crew, however, we can really go places.

Throughout our life, we will encounter many different "crews"—college friends, softball buddies, neighbors, faith groups. But as we grow and move to new places, not everyone comes with us. Who are the people who do? The crew I'm talking about is your inner circle. This is the group of people who have the greatest capacity and influence to help you grow; to expand your self-awareness, strengths, and talents; to open you to all the possibilities of living your passion and finding your purpose. These are the people who will stick by you through ups and downs (and you by them), the people who will gladly take a call from you at 3:00 a.m., those whom you enjoy being around and have *fun* with, who feed your soul with laughter and enjoyment. You share a close, trusted bond because you can be vulnerable with them and truly yourself.

You often form strong, trusting relationships with those who share many of your values or passions, who acknowledge your strengths and accept your vulnerabilities, who have your best interests at heart. But for your personal growth, it is critically important that you embrace diverse perspectives and feedback. If your inner circle doesn't have the right mix of personalities and perspectives, you can close yourself off to a variety of experiences and life-changing opportunities, and you risk developing blind spots. It is hard to achieve true self-awareness when you cannot fully "know thyself."

For this reason, you must learn to withhold judgment from others and open yourself to diverse ways of thinking, various walks of life, and different socioeconomic and cultural backgrounds. You want to bring into your inner circle individuals who challenge your thinking so that you gain a deeper understanding of yourself and others. You can't cultivate a 360-degree view of the world when you only look at it from your own narrow angle.

To break through these artificial boundaries, you need a strong and empathetic crew—those folks you trust with your life, who build you up, who give you loving feedback, and who impact your life in positive ways. We cannot do it alone, and our inner circle will be there to nurture us and help us learn what it truly means to grab the helm.

LOUIS

Monday morning Louis arrived at the office promptly at 7:30. How many more Mondays did he have? He was retiring in two weeks, so two more? That was it? When you put it like that... *I guess this is really happening*, he thought.

He had been CFO for more than twenty of his forty-five years with the company and had forgone the corner office that would have been his, turning it into a media room that had evolved over the years, first as a copy room, then as a copy/printing room, then as a training room, and now as high-tech studio for video and podcasting. He liked to joke that he had no idea what went on in that room anymore, but that was disingenuous—he had been the one to approve the funding for its buildout, and he never approved funding without understanding the ins and outs of the project. He wasn't a Scrooge with funds; he just liked to know what he was paying for.

Louis's office was one of the managers' offices, just off the corner, with a large window that looked out on the bullpen. The actual managers were out on the floor with the team leads and the team members in the open floor plan—accounting and bookkeeping, accounts payable, accounts receivable, audit, financial planning and budgeting, payroll. Rebecca from financial planning was taking over as CFO when he left. She was already performing most of the day-to-day tasks. Everyone kept telling Louis to take it easy, but he wasn't very good at being idle. In fact, in addition to packing up his office, he was preparing one last report—a ten-year plan—for the executive team and the board. Truth be told, he was working more on the report than packing the office. He had gotten as far as bringing in the banker's boxes, which he had stacked neatly along the wall—empty.

He pulled his laptop out of the battered leather messenger bag Madeline had given him when he first became CFO, popped it into the docking station, and booted up. He sorted through the paper files and envelopes in his inbox, and once he had access to the computer, he opened the report and scrolled through it. It was like hundreds he had done in his time there, and that was the problem: it was all the usual text and graphics. He wondered if he could get another set of eyes to help him out.

Someone banged on the picture window. The blinds were retracted, as usual, so he could look out on his team, and there was Rebecca, leather portfolio in one hand, silver commuter mug in the other. The morning team meeting. He grabbed the agenda from his inbox, patted the pocket of his blazer to make sure he had a pen, then followed her to the executive conference room, the name of which was a tired joke, since there was only one conference room on the floor.

When he walked in the room, he felt the hum of his team's quiet energy. They almost always seemed to want to be there, even on a Monday morning. This was one of his proudest accomplishments, putting this group together. Rebecca from planning, more visionary than accountant; her assistant, Tanaka, who would take over when Rebecca replaced Louis; Phil from accounts receivable, who wouldn't let an invoice go uncollected; Tiffany from payroll, who had mastered—indeed invented—their complex system of commissions and bonuses; Sarah from accounting, whom they called the watchmaker because she was so precise; Sam in audit, the Rock due to his tenacity. Some of the team he had brought up through the department; others he had pulled in from outside. They were the reason he hadn't had much to do the last year or so and gave him the assurance to finally put in for retirement.

Louis went to sit in one of the side seats, but Rebecca, who was still standing, said, "Don't you dare. You're at the head of the table until the day you leave."

Louis capitulated, not wanting to cause a fuss. But it was Rebecca's meeting, and she ran it efficiently, as he had taught her. There was no cross chatter, and no one was looking at their phones or tablets except to jot a note here or there. He wanted to interject a few times, but he held his tongue—that was their agreement—because she usually worked her way around to what he was going to say anyway. Which she did that day just fine.

They had worked their way down to the last item, a big fat question mark. Everyone, including Louis, looked in anticipation at Rebecca. She made one last note about the previous item, then raised her head and smiled. "All right, Louis. Out you go. Your presence is not required for this last one."

He looked around the table sternly, as if he was about to give them all one of his quiet dressing downs. Some of the newer folks actually sat back in their chairs, expecting one. Then he wryly lifted one corner of his mouth.

"Ah, yes, the surprise party. You can't have me around to talk about that."

"Don't know what you're talking about," Rebecca said, straight faced. "It's just some low-level stuff. We figured you'd want to get back to your office and fill some of those boxes…"

"About that," he said, his face growing even more serious. He stood up. "Manuel and I have been talking. He's planning a huge initiative next year and asked me to stick around to see it through. It's a two-phase rollout, might take twelve to eighteen months. It appears that rumors of my retirement have been greatly exaggerated."

The team gaped at him in stunned silence. Then all at once they burst into chatter.

"But it was announced—"

"Manuel said—"

"What about Becca and Tanaka—"

"Are you serious?"

He looked around the room, holding each one of them with quiet command. "No," he said, breaking into a huge smile. "I'm not serious. I'm still leaving in two weeks."

They waited a beat to make sure they had it right this time, then burst out in laughter.

"Man, you guys are easy." He stood up. "The looks on your faces when you thought I was staying. I think I should be offended. Seriously, though, no big fuss, okay? You know me. A card and a cupcake. I may not have much to do, but I know you do."

"Whatever you say, *boss*. Card and a cupcake. Now shoo," said Rebecca.

He made to leave, then turned back to the table. "One thing, though. And this is real. I need some help with this last report I'm putting together. Anyone have any bright young folks who might be able to?"

"Qasim," several of them said at the same time, then looked at each other.

"Qasim? I don't think I know him."

"He's been here a couple of months—a hard person not to notice." Tanaka said. "Highly energetic. Very bright. Very… very…" He paused. "You'll see what we mean."

He looked at them, trying to figure out if they were getting back at him for his joke. But they seemed sincere enough. "Qasim it is. Send him over."

JIM

The house turned out to be in one of those old city neighborhoods with huge Victorians taking up a whole block of their own. Hedges as high as basketball poles surrounded the yards, and driveways and sidewalks were cracked and upended by the roots of huge knotty trees like something out of *The Lord of the Rings*.

This wouldn't have been Jim and Shauna's choice. They had built both of their homes new, preferring to move into houses that were clean and unlived in, with Jim having a lot to say about the design and the landscaping. These old giants were a homeowner's nightmare but a renovator's dream—and since today and for the next few weeks he was a renovator, he guessed he should be grateful.

Jim pulled in behind Patricia's old white Ford F-250. She had bought it used shortly after college and had held on to it so long it must be a classic by now. But classic or not, it was a work truck, with a steel rack for tools and lumber above the bed, rusting dents in the tailgate, and a yellow right front quarter panel. From what Jim knew, her business was successful enough for her to buy a whole fleet of new trucks, which he often tried to sell her from the dealership. That wasn't her style, though.

In front of Pat's truck and on the other side of the street were parked some older compacts and hatchbacks that must have belonged to the rest of the crew. Automatically, he began to think of how to approach the car owners to interest them in a newer Toyota, then laughed at himself. That was his *other* job.

The crew gathered in front of a three-car garage built to look like a barn. Good. They looked like they were all early. He was a navy man. If you were on time, you were late. Pat must have remembered that. What *he* had to remember was that this was Pat's company, not his team at the dealership. He adjusted the straps on the carpenter's overalls he had pulled out of his workshop closet and headed toward the group.

Pat, a tall, broad-shouldered woman with shoulder-length blond hair now shading to gray, was chatting with the group. She wore her own construction gear.

When she saw Jim walking up the driveway, she turned to welcome him. The other three shuffled to the side to let him in the circle. "Hey, Jimbo," she called to him, his college nickname. She was the only one who called him that anymore. Then she turned to the group. "This is the Jim I was telling you about. Your crew chief for this job. He knows what he's doing, but it's been a while, so he might need some help with some of the logistics—how we order supplies, how to keep track of hours and materials, that sort of thing." To Jim she said, "We do it on a tablet these days. Insane." Then, to one of the crew, a thin, dark-haired young man with a sleeve of tattoos on either arm and a bull ring in his nose, she said, "Thien, you help him out, okay?"

"Sure," the young man said.

"Thien's been around awhile, so he knows how it works. He's up to date on the codes too. He's good with design." Pat held out the tablet.

Jim stepped in and took it himself. "I'm sure I'll be able to figure it out."

Pat looked at him as if she was about to say something, then said, "Okay. Just trying to streamline things."

Thien shrugged.

"Here's the rest of the crew." She gestured toward a young woman with dyed black hair and black lipstick who seemed no older than Dionne. "Amanda is our wrecking crew. She likes to destroy things. Knows her way around a crowbar." Amanda raised the well-used crowbar she held in her hand. "She's also one of our best painters. And here's Ken," she said, indicating someone who, at about six feet, two hundred pounds, finally looked like he belonged on a construction crew. "He's good at carrying things."

Ken grimaced when she said this.

Pat grinned. "I love doing that to him. He's really an electrician and a plumber, so he might come in handy in that old basement."

At that moment, the garage door opened, and there stood an older woman in a business suit, authoritative and well put together.

Pat said, "And this is Madeline, the lady of the house."

"Oh, Patricia, aren't you sweet. No one has called me a lady for quite a while." They hugged warmly.

Pat said, "Madeline, this is Jim. He'll be in charge of the renovation."

"Old friends?" Jim asked, reaching out his hand.

"Just met a few weeks ago," Madeline said, shaking his hand. "Nice to meet you. Once you get going, if you need anything, let me know. All right. I'm headed to some kind of meeting where they'll probably ask me to chair something or write a check or both. You have the keys and the security code, right?"

"Yes, ma'am," Pat said.

"All right. If the house falls in, call my husband. Have a great day."

They stepped aside as she returned to her luxury SUV and backed out of the driveway.

Pat said to the crew, "You guys unload the truck while I fill in Jim here."

Pat took Jim into the basement and showed him the preliminary plans on the tablet, but reminded him that she had pegged him for this job for his creativity and he could change things around, with the client's permission, of course. They walked around the basement. Structurally, it seemed to be in good shape, but it was definitely outdated. They had their hands full.

"I've got to get to the downtown site. Anything else?"

"Well, uh, the crew. You sure about them? They look more like a rock band."

"If I didn't hire workers with tattoos and facial jewelry, I'd go out of business. But they're great and know their stuff. They're not crazy about micromanagement, though, if you know what I mean." Pat squeezed him on the arm, then banged her way up the stairs, after which Thien, Amanda, and Ken pounded their way down.

"Gather up," Jim said. "First step, demolition. Ken, you start tearing down that old paneling on the walls. Thien, you measure the space around the fireplace. Oh, and you, Amanda, why don't you just kind of clean up after Ken, throw all that stuff into the dumpster."

Thien spoke up. "Uh, Mr., uh—"

"Jim, just call me Jim."

"Jim, then. Amanda usually—"

"Let's just do it my way, okay? That's what I'm here for."

They all looked at each other, shrugged, and went to work.

Jim paced the room with the tablet in his hand, comparing the drawings to what he had in mind. After a half hour of this, he was ready to make his changes on the drawings, except—these were electronic. How hard could it be? There was a stylus, and this was a tablet, right? Only, once he detached the stylus and started to draw on the screen, nothing happened. He shook the stylus, pressed it to the screen. Then he brought the screen to his face and examined it closely. He pressed the screen, moved his fingers like he was finger painting, but all he seemed to manage was to smear his prints across the surface. As a last resort, he shook the tablet out of frustration more than anything else. He didn't really think that would do anything.

"It's not an Etch A Sketch."

Jim jumped. Thien was standing next to him. Jim wondered how long he had been there. "I'm surprised you even know what that is."

"My parents saved all their childhood stuff."

"I would have thought—"

"They were immigrants because of my name and how I look? I'm fourth generation, actually. May I?"

He held out his hand. Jim handed him the tablet and then the stylus. Thien tapped the screen a few times, then turned it back toward Jim. "It was in view mode so you can't make changes by mistake. If you click Edit, you'll be able to make changes. Press Save to save the changes. The app has a cool feature that automatically renames each new version. Press View to read the plans with the new changes. Use View and Edit to toggle back and forth." He demonstrated and looked at Jim.

"Thank you. I guess I couldn't figure it out on my own."

"May I make another suggestion? I mean, while we're working so well together?" Thien said, not trying to hide his sarcasm.

"Yeah, sure," Jim said.

"Look over there." He pointed to where Ken and Amanda were tearing down the old paneling. Only a small section of the wall was completed.

"I thought they'd be farther than that."

"They would be if—"

"If?"

"If you let Amanda tear it down. She really does like to destroy things, and she's good at it. Ken likes to put things together."

"Pat did say that. I thought she was joking."

"Pat likes to joke around, but she knows her people."

"What about you?" Jim said.

"I usually just tell the boss what to do."

"I see," Jim said. "What should I do?"

"You mean after you tell Ken and Amanda to switch jobs?"

"Right."

"I finished the fireplace measurements. We can talk about restoring the mantel."

"Perfect," Jim said. He went over to Ken and Amanda and told them he had it on good authority that they should switch jobs. They both smiled. Amanda grabbed the crowbar from Ken's hand, and in thirty seconds stripped a section of the wall almost as big as the one they had been working on for half an hour.

Then Jim huddled with Thien to discuss the mantel. They found themselves in agreement about most things—what to keep and restore, what to have Amanda rip out and replace. Madeline and her husband had given them a lot of liberty. Jim wanted to keep the wood dark but with more of a sheen. Thien wanted to lighten it. Jim wasn't sure about the TV Thien wanted to hide behind a retractable panel above the fireplace. He told Thien to run the numbers on heat proofing for the electronics and maybe he'd consider it.

In the afternoon, they all pitched in to haul out the debris Amanda so effectively produced. Ken had rigged up a conveyor belt that carried the debris out one of the basement windows to the side yard near the dumpster. They rotated their stations from the basement to the dumpster without even discussing it.

Before Jim knew it, the tablet beeped twice, then let loose with the sound of an old-time factory whistle. Jim laughed. "I'm guessing that was you, Thien."

"Tomorrow I'll bring the Etch A Sketch."

Amanda ripped out one more two-by-four, then dropped her crowbar.

"It's a day," Jim said, reaching his arms above his head to stretch his back and shoulders. He didn't know the last time a work day had gone so fast, though he was looking forward to a nice hot shower, and he knew he was going to sleep well that night. They had made great progress, and the next day they could get started on patching the rock walls and installing the framework for the new paneling.

"Okay, before we go, gather around. Please." They moved in closer than he thought they would. Nothing like hard physical labor to bring a team together. "First, thank you. I'm the new guy here, and after a bit of a rough start, you brought me along just fine. Now, I used to play some football…"

Out of the corner of his eye Jim saw Thien slap a five-dollar bill in Amanda's hand while she mouthed "I told you."

"…and we used to do this at the end of every practice. It's kind of fun. Put your hands in the middle—you know what I'm talking about, right, Ken?"

"Not really. I was on the golf team in high school. We were pretty laid back."

"Oh, I thought—never mind." He'd really have to work on his assumptions. Or just give them up altogether. "Okay. We count one-two-three, raise our hands, and yell out 'Team.' Who wants the count?"

They all looked at each other, then, to Jim's surprise, Amanda said, "I'll do it."

Jim nodded, but since she hadn't said three words all day, he was ready to jump in to help. "One. Two. Three," Amanda called out with much more authority than Jim had expected, and they all shot their hands in the air and joined in for a resounding "Team!"

It had been a day of surprises, and Jim was looking forward to more to come.

JANELLE

Janelle settled in nervously for her first class: Jazz Ensemble with Professor Muñoz, an accomplished jazz musician in her early sixties who had mostly stopped touring to teach in the program. Janelle had done her research.

She took an open seat near the front. It was still thirty minutes before class, and the classroom was nearly full. Not only was everyone else likely to be a better musician than she was, apparently they were more eager as well. She should have arrived earlier.

She placed her music on the stand in front of her chair, but a few pages fluttered to the floor. As she scrambled to pick them up, she glanced around the room. Dionne was already chatting in the back with the other keyboard players. Why couldn't Janelle be outgoing like that? A few other string players to her right were engaged in small talk—what they had done over the summer, who sold the best pizza, was there a good vegan restaurant in town. Janelle didn't know much about any of that, so she replaced the music on her stand and did what she did best—observed.

After a minute, another woman—silky dark hair to her neck, big brown eyes, skin just a shade lighter than Janelle's own—sat in the empty chair to Janelle's left and unpacked her bag. She managed to put her music on the stand without the fuss Janelle had made.

Janelle took a deep breath and looked up. Here was her chance. "I've been practicing that all week. I can't really get the last page quite right, but hopefully we'll go over it today."

The woman looked her over briefly, wrinkled her nose, and returned to organizing her things. "We played that piece in high school," she said flatly.

"Not us." Janelle dog-eared one corner of the sheet music, then smoothed it back again. "We had a pretty small program. We were lucky we didn't have to practice in the parking lot." When the dark-haired woman didn't laugh or follow up, Janelle went on. "I'm Janelle."

"Padme Darvish." She said her name as if she thought Janelle should know who she was. When Janelle didn't respond on cue, Padme continued with some disdain, "My family has been part of this program for years."

The name did sound familiar, Janelle thought as she sorted through the possibilities. Then it hit her. "The Darvish Performance Center," she said aloud. "That's you?"

"My grandfather," she said, stone faced. When she turned to the students on the other side of her, though, her face lit up in recognition, and they chatted about the summer programs they must have all attended together.

So it's just me Padme detests, Janelle thought. She glanced back at Dionne, who was engrossed in conversation and didn't notice her. Janelle stared at her sheet music, only just successful in fighting back the tears that threatened to erupt when she was unsure and overwhelmed.

Things smoothed out once Professor Muñoz arrived and they got involved in the details of the class—the syllabus, what the work would look like, how the grades were decided.

At the end of the class they drew lots for performance times, which made Janelle nervous all over again.

They only had the one class that day. They were expected to use the bulk of their time for study and practice, Janelle supposed. She guessed she was expected to do a lot of this on her own. She had always thought she was independent and showed strong initiative, but she had to admit that she felt a little lost. Dionne had found some friends she had known from the camps she had attended all her life. Apparently the world of elite musicians was a small one when you had been playing since the age of four. Despite the item on her to-do list to be more social, Janelle begged off when Dionne asked her to go to lunch with her old friends. She was feeling a little sorry for herself. She walked over to the performance center to check out the practice rooms instead, and there it was in huge letters on the face of the modern structure: Darvish Performance Center. She'd better get used to it now, she thought. It was going to be in her face the rest of her time here.

There was a set of turnstiles for the general audience on performance nights, she guessed, and another turnstile next to a glass-enclosed guard station with a sign that read Faculty and Students. She had done this hundreds of times at other venues and places of work, so she slid her ID through the card reader and pushed the turnstile all in one motion, then bent double as if she had been punched in the stomach. It wouldn't let her through. She must have gone too fast. She backed up and tried again, with the same result. Was this a message from the universe? She heard a banging at the attendant station, looked that way. A youngish red-haired man dressed in a security uniform waved her over. She backed out of the lane and went to the window, which had a round speaker for talking and a shallow silver tray.

"Let me see your ID," the man said through the tinny speaker and pointed to the tray. He was professionally pleasant, at least. Janelle complied. He examined the ID back and front, then propped it next to his keyboard, typed, and read the screen. Satisfied with what he saw, he slid the card through a strip reader on the keyboard, shook his head, pushed the card back to her through the tray. "It should work. You're in the system, and that picture is definitely you, unless you're the evil twin."

Janelle didn't say anything.

"That kind of day, huh? I think it's the magnetic strip. Go back to the registrar and ask for a new card."

She slapped the card into her hand and turned to leave.

"But I can let you in. Your ID is still valid."

She turned back to face the window. "I'm sorry," she said, genuinely grateful. "It *has* been a day. You've been great. I think I'll just get this taken care of before things get even crazier."

"Cheer up! Before you know it, I'll be letting people in to see you perform."

He must have read on the ID that she was in the program. She cracked a small smile. "I wouldn't be too sure, the way things are going."

"Nah, I can see it in your eyes. You'll be on that stage in no time."

"Thanks again," she said, and pulled out her campus map to find the registrar's office.

At the registrar's office, she stood in the line of people with first-day snafus like hers, and finally got her card taken care of. They assured her the magnetic strip on this one worked, and they actually apologized. The woman at the counter explained that a bad batch of blank cards had been shipped to them by their vendor, and some of the cards had been processed before they figured it out.

That actually made her feel better—it didn't seem as much of an omen. By the time she got back to the apartment, she was in a lighter mood. Just a hiccup on the road to success! *At least that was my last first day of school*, Janelle told herself. *Unless I fail and decide to become a lawyer…or get a PhD. Okay, one step at a time.*

She was surprised to see that Dionne had beaten her home. She had just assumed that, as outgoing as Dionne was, Janelle would, for all intents and purposes, be living alone. But there was Dionne, on the couch in the middle of a circle of folders and papers and notebooks and her keyboard on the cushion next to her. Dionne had no trouble settling in.

"Hey, roomie." Dionne jumped up from the couch, her things cascading to the floor, and practically skipped over to Janelle, then stopped, and opened her arms wide for a hug.

Janelle thought over her day, then nodded and collapsed into Dionne's arms. Things didn't seem quite so bad anymore.

"How'd you feel about the first day?" Dionne asked.

"Oh, fine," she said. "It was fine."

"That bad?"

"I hope people warm up a bit. You think they will?"

"No." Dionne laughed. "I mean, it's music school—all that *Sturm und Drang*. We're supposed to be solitary titans shaking our fists at an indifferent universe."

This made Janelle smile. "I don't know. I do like to stay by myself a bit, as you may have noticed—"

Dionne mimed, *No, really*—

"But I used to be a big soccer player—all through college, actually."

"No way. Didn't all those people drive you crazy?"

"The opposite. I liked having that team dynamic as a release. You know, work hard, play hard, there for each other through thick and thin—the really bad games and killer practices, and the big wins. There was such a sense of camaraderie. You don't feel so…solitary, as you put it. I've had soccer all my life. I'm going to miss it, I think."

"I know what you mean. But hey, it's the first day of school. Who enjoys the first day of school? We'll build our own team, you and me. Honestly, if things go well on the first day, that's when you should worry."

"I guess."

"Interesting that you played soccer."

"Yeah, for like twelve years. I was captain my last two."

"Captain? Wow."

"We were a small school. But I liked that role. I think I'd hate it in any other context. That makes sense, right?"

Dionne nodded. "Yeah, sure—it was something you were good at and people you were comfortable with. I felt the same way with my band."

"Your band? You mean like the college concert band?"

"No, my *band*. Dionne and the Deltoids. We did some of the local bars and clubs, filled in for an AWOL opening act every once in a while at the bigger venues. Here's some pictures." She unlocked her phone, scrolled through the pictures, handed it to Janelle, then scooted so they were shoulder-to-shoulder.

In the picture Janelle saw a very made-up Dionne with rock-star hair and a glittery top, posing at a piano and a microphone. "Wow. Dionne, you look—stunning. Did you actually sing?"

"Oh, yeah, we all did. I sang the pop stuff. Mick—that's

his real name, no lie—sang rock 'n' roll, and Rory, he did the ballads. What a sweet voice. That boy could break your heart in four notes. It was fun," she said wistfully. "And we made some money too—decent money for people still living with their parents, anyway."

"What happened?"

"Well, this program, for one. There's way more I want to learn about music. And you know, it got a little boring playing to crowds who are only there to eat and drink and chat up potential dates rather than listen to us. It was time to move on."

"I never could have done that."

"What are you talking about? You'd be great. That's what we were missing—a good fiddle player." Dionne winked.

Janelle spoke through her nose like she was a grande dame in an old movie. "I don't play *fiddle*, I play violin."

"What*ever*," Dionne said, then they both laughed. "So don't sweat it. I'm a little turned around too, a little homesick. But don't think for a second I'm going to tell my father that." She wagged her finger.

"Your secret's safe with me."

"Okay, so here's the deal. I'll be your soccer team, you be my band, and it's down the yellow brick road for us."

"You mixed, like, fifteen metaphors right there."

It was Dionne's turn to be the grande dame. "You exaggerate, my dear." Then in her normal voice she said, "Let's grab a bite. Take our mind off things." Dionne put her arm out. Janelle put her arm through Dionne's, and once they maneuvered through the door, Dionne broke out in, "We're off to see the wizard…"

For the first time since she arrived—well, truthfully, for the first time since she received her acceptance last spring—Janelle didn't feel as if she had to do this all on her own.

Reflection and Activity

None of our characters are going it alone. Each is part of a crew—more than one crew, really—larger groups within which they are conducting their purpose.

Louis is proud of the finance team he put together to keep the firm running smoothly. Further, his wife, Madeline, is part of his home nucleus, as is his granddaughter, Janelle. He's leaving his work family behind when he retires, however. Is he going to form a new crew to carry him forward?

Like Louis, Jim has a strong home crew in his wife, Shauna, and daughter, Dionne. When he begins Pat's project, however, he faces a new team the likes of which he hasn't seen before. It takes a good deal of openness and self-awareness for Jim to adapt, but by the end of the day, they all come together.

Janelle misses her soccer team and has doubts that she will find a new crew among the competitive and distant musicians in her program. This contributes to her self-doubts and loneliness. Her outgoing roommate, Dionne, cheers her up by saying, "Let's form a crew of two."

Who is your crew, your inner circle? Who are the individuals you are closest to? You can define closeness in whatever way you like, but it is helpful to think of your crew as the individuals you trust the most, those you are willing to be vulnerable with and take feedback from, those you can call any time day or night and they'll pick up. These are the people you rely on the most.

Reflect on your crew and then jot down a list of your crew members. This is just for you, so feel free to use names, initials, whatever you like. Once you finish, draw a circle, then think of which of these people belong in your innermost circle. Who would you put in that tight, intimate group right in the center? Then draw another circle around the first one, leaving space for more names. Who is in that next circle? These are likely people you are still close to, but with whom you don't share the same level of trust. Keep going outward in concentric circles with as many or as few circles as make sense in your life.

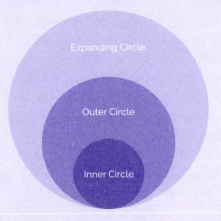

The different levels are often determined by different areas of your life: your partner, immediate family, extended family, best friends, casual friends, acquaintances, club or sport team members, parents of your children's friends, team members at work. Are you as close to the people at work as you are to your best friends? You might be, if you work with your best friends, but more often work teams consist of people you don't choose for yourself. That doesn't mean you can't work well and effectively with them, and even be friendly, but you may not confide in them in a personal way. The same with sports teams or quilting clubs or yoga classes. People can cross over into more than one group, of course, and you can certainly meet someone who becomes part of your inner circle in any of these groups. What's important is to not mistake a casual acquaintance, for example, for someone in your inner circle. That can lead to confusion and even hurt feelings.

To figure out whether someone belongs in your crew, ask yourself: How does your individual helm connect with that person's individual helm? Do you share the same values? The same passions? Do your purposes align? Perhaps you have the same talents or, even better, complementary talents.

Remember the child's game with the gears we mentioned in the introduction? If you think of each gear as the helm of a person in your circles of trust, then the gears closer to you affect you more often and more directly than the ones further out, just as you affect the ones closest to you more often and more directly. But remember that everyone is connected and affects everyone else in large and small ways. This is where your individual helm connects to the larger organizational helm— and here we don't just mean work organizations, we mean any group of people trying to achieve a common goal: teams, clubs, families, boards, and so on. Individual helms working in concert with other individuals and their helms can do great things.

Once you're satisfied with the names in your circles, take inventory. Look for patterns and associations. Of the people you wrote down, is everyone the same? Does everyone share the exact same values and philosophies? Having things in common is important, of course, even necessary, but if everyone in your circle is a clone of each other, you might fall into a mindset of groupthink that hinders openness and growth. Do you have the right mix of people who will *really* challenge you to open up to greater possibilities? A good crew raises you up, they don't bring you down. You raise each other up.

To return to the sailing metaphor, if I'm a good navigator, and I set sail with a bunch of other good navigators, we likely will all know where we are going, but will we be able to get there? On a boat you need a variety of people with a range of talents—someone good at navigation, someone strong at the helm, someone good in the galley, someone who knows electronics and engines, someone who can arrange the sails. The person standing watch on the stern gives you a much different perspective than the one at the bow.

I'm not telling you to draft your inner circle the way a GM drafts a professional sports team. What I am suggesting is to be self-aware enough to open yourself to other personalities and perspectives in your inner circle. Remember the four color energies we discussed in the chapter on self-awareness? If you're finding that your crew is all one shade, then think about embracing other personality colors. (See how all the spokes work together?)

And don't forget to practice gratitude for those you have on your crew right now—partners, family, friends, mentors, work teams. They've helped you get this far.

Go to www.grabthehelm.com to enter your reflections and access more information.

CHAPTER 5

THE FIFTH SPOKE OF THE HELM
PASSION

*There is no passion to be found playing small—
in settling for a life that is less than the one
you are capable of living.*
—Nelson Mandela

What do you get up early for? What do you stay up late for? What do you just love to do? What activities do you dive into and before you know it, half the day has gone by? These are your passions.

Passion is the foundation of Leading from the Helm. Passion is what drives us to do the things we do—to pursue our purpose. Passion is the wind in our sails, the fuel that motivates us, what feeds our soul. Passion gives us energy. For the purposes of Leading from the Helm, I'm talking about the big passions, the passions that drive our pursuit of purpose. Sure, we can have a passion for peanut butter, but unless we own a peanut butter factory, peanut butter isn't likely to be a life-driving passion. But there's the lesson. Though peanut butter may not be *your* life-driving passion, it could be someone else's.

One of the problems we run into with passions is that many of us feel as if we don't have the time to explore them, that pursuing our passions is somehow self-indulgent. The practicalities of daily life get in the way: working to earn money for food and shelter, taking care of our families, doing housework or yard work, cooking meals, washing dishes, visiting relatives. But when we fill our life only with activities and tasks for which we have little or no passion, life becomes a burden. Life without passion is an obligation and a duty and is simply not sustainable.

For this reason, it is critical that you tap into passion every day. Otherwise, life will simply grind you down. We all have duties and obligations. The trick is to learn how to keep our tank full so we can do the things for which we have little passion (and do them well so we can stand tall) and still have something left over for what we are passionate about. But here's the good news about passion: pursuing our passions is what keeps our tanks full.

Of course, we must pursue our passions responsibly, without hurting others (and ourselves)—those closest to us and the community at large. Left unchecked, our passions can turn into obsessions. How do we combine our passions with our talents to be fruitful and serve others? How do we become self-aware enough to align our passions with our values? Passion may be the foundational spoke of Leading from the Helm, but it works in concert with all the others.

If we feel drained of passion, it could very well be because we are so dedicated to fulfilling our obligations that we don't even know what our passions are anymore—if we ever did. If we have been living without passion for so long, the first step may be to give ourselves permission to explore what we are passionate about. It's critical that we become self-aware about our passions, for they may be hiding behind unexpected doors. We need to bravely try new things and venture outside of our comfort zone to tap into our hidden passions. The exercises at the end of the chapter will help you recognize what you love to do, steer you toward what gives you joy, and inspire you to open yourself to your true passions.

LOUIS

Louis was in his office scrolling through his report when a dark-haired young man appeared just outside his door. Probably an intern looking for the restrooms, Louis said to himself, going back to his screen. There was something missing in the report, and he couldn't put his finger on it. He leaned back and looked at the ceiling, his classic thinking pose. He noticed the young man was still loitering around the door.

"Can I help you?"

Once Louis acknowledged him, the man lit up and shot into the office. "I'm supposed to help *you*, I think." He made his way around the desk and squeezed in next to Louis. "Is that the report they're talking about? No wonder you need my help. Words and numbers. Nobody's going to read that."

"Hold on a minute," Louis said, hitting the key for his screensaver. "Proprietary information. Other side of the desk, please." He waved him over.

"Oh, yeah, sorry, we do that all the time out on the floor."
He moved in front of the desk.

"In this office we introduce ourselves before we do anything else. I'm Louis. Chief financial officer."

"I know who you are," the young man practically snorted. "I'm Qasim. They said you needed some help with a report or something." He rocked back and forth, then sideways.

"Ah, Qasim, they did mention your name. Would you like to have a seat while we get to know each other?" Louis indicated the small round table with two chairs in one corner of his office next to the stack of boxes.

"No, that's all right. I like to stand."

"Please, sit," Louis said, walking over to the table and pulling out a chair.

Qasim sat, looked around the room nervously, his feet still pumping on the floor. He was dressed as most of the team dressed, in khakis and a polo shirt. The sneakers he was wearing, however, were not regulation.

Louis decided to let it go. "What makes you think you can help?"

"I majored in business analytics and minored in computer graphic design at Harvey University. This is literally what I do."

"You went to Harvey? That's my alma mater."

"Yeah, I know. That's why I'm here. I mean, at this company. You gave a talk my freshman year as part of the orientation about your passion for numbers and how you didn't get much support as a kid until you got to Harvey. I looked for you every year since, but I must have missed you."

"That was a one-time deal—a favor for a friend. The dean."

"You were awesome. You should do that every year. You made it sound exciting working at this company. I vowed to apply here if I graduated."

"*If* you graduated? Was there a problem?"

"Only with tuition, not classes. I loved the classes. I couldn't get enough. Mom was a single mother, and she worked hard, but there wasn't a lot for extras. I patched together a couple of scholarships and worked in the dining hall all four years and picked up other odd jobs, factory work in the summer. I kept looking for that one fellowship that would carry me through, but I never found it. But I did it. I graduated, and here I am." He looked around the room. "What's with the boxes?"

"I'm retiring. You may have heard."

"Ah, right. I did hear. And right when I get here too. Bad news for me. What are you doing next? Have you decided?"

Louis looked sharply at the young man who had barely stopped for breath. Qasim had no lack of passion. "Not really, no."

"Well, at least go back and do those freshman talks. Those were really inspiring. And they bring a lot of speakers in for classes and other events. You'd be good at that too."

"Thanks for the advice," Louis said dryly.

"No problem," Qasim responded, not catching the irony.

When Louis thought about it, though, there was no reason he couldn't learn something from someone so young. He learned from his granddaughter all the time. He stood up. "Shall we take a look at the report?"

Qasim leapt from his chair. "Let's do it."

Did I ever have that much energy? Louis wondered. "One

second," Louis said, grabbing a pen and scratch pad from his desk. He wrote "Speeches?" and "Fellowship?" in big letters on the page. He felt a tug of inspiration. He wasn't sure where it would lead, but he had an inkling of what his next passion might be. Then he turned to Qasim and said, "Okay. Let's see what you've got."

JIM

Patricia had needed the rest of the crew for the huge complex they were starting on the other side of town, so Jim was by himself in the basement doing some of the finish work. He couldn't remember a time when he'd felt more invigorated and engaged. Well, that wasn't completely true. This was how he always felt when he was working with his hands, whether on his kids' tree house or with Pat all those years ago—before he came up in the world, he snorted to himself. When he was working on a house or a yard or a room, he became one with the job in a way he never had as a sales manager. He couldn't really lose himself in the work at the dealership the way he could building things. It was like the days he and his pals had spent sunrise to sunset in the woods around the house he grew up in, "exploring," as they called it, and building forts, and playing games. This was what he meant when he'd called Pat's job "too much fun." It bordered on self-indulgent. Wasn't work supposed to be hard? That was what he had always been taught by the adults in his life.

And he liked building things for others—that was part of the pleasure. Sure, he enjoyed building the shelves and workbenches for his own garage, but seeing the wide-eyed joy in the kids' eyes when he unveiled the tree house was something he'd never forget, as well as the satisfaction in the old days when one of Pat's customers told them, "How did you do that? That's exactly how I imagined it!" The passion, the joy of creation, was deeper when you shared it. A home was so much more than a house, and that was something Jim could provide. Not everyone could.

Not that he wasn't feeling it when he went home at night. He was using muscles he hadn't used in a while, and after watching TV with Shauna, he ached all over—but it was a good ache, the ache of accomplishment. A long hot shower had never felt so good. Was this how Dionne felt after a concert? He'd have to ask her the next time they talked. And the sleep. He hadn't slept this deeply in years. He woke up restored and ready to go.

What would his life have been like if he had stuck with construction? Less secure, that was for sure. A long time ago Pat had offered him part of the company if he stuck around. But he had already met Shauna, they were planning a family, and he was making a good living at the dealership. He hadn't wanted to roll the dice on the uncertainties of the construction world.

But now what was holding him back? Maybe doing this work was just the grass-is-greener syndrome, and if construction was his full-time job, he'd get as tired of it as he was of the dealership. He didn't really believe that, but it was possible. No, this kind of worked aligned with his passion. He had never understood that whole "follow your bliss" thing, but maybe this was it. Passion, bliss, engagement, losing yourself in your work. All the same thing, really. Didn't he deserve a piece of that? Didn't everybody? He recalled with regret some of the recent "discussions" he had had with Dionne in which he had questioned her life choices. Something else to talk about the next time they spoke.

Did he really want to spend the rest of his life doing something he only half liked? He was barely middle-aged, yet he was beginning to feel old—except when he was doing this, remodeling, working with his hands. This work was the fountain of youth for him. Could he make up for lost time? Or was he too late?

This had been the danger of taking this job all along: that he'd get a taste of what he was missing and grow even more dissatisfied with what he was doing. That he would go back to his old life with regrets. But what if he did do this for the rest of his life? Their kids were grown, he and Shauna had very little debt except the mortgage, they already had some decent retirement savings. Nah, he couldn't. Could he?

Not without Shauna on board. He finished installing the baseboards along the far wall, then checked his watch. Four o'clock. Shauna should be alone in her classroom, her kids dismissed for the day. She'd be prepping the next day's classes and correcting papers. They didn't like to interrupt each other at work, but he had to talk to her about this.

"Jim?" Shauna answered, surprised. "Is everything all right? Did you get hurt?"

"No, no, nothing like that. I've just been thinking…"

"Ah," she said. "What are you thinking about?"

"Are you ready for an adventure?"

"Every day's an adventure with you, my love."

"Ha ha. I love you too." He smiled. "No, I've been thinking about what you said—you know, when you talked me into doing this project for Pat."

"*Encouraged* you. I encouraged you take this project with Pat. You made the call all on your own. What did I say again?"

"You said…that I owe it to myself, and to you guys, to go after my passion after all these years at the dealership. That's what I've been thinking about. How would I do that? How would that look?"

"Assuming we're talking about remodeling houses and not some other midlife crisis like touring the country in an RV, then how *would* it look?"

"No, no RV." He laughed again. "Picture this: 'Bulldog Fine Home Remodeling.'" He raised his hand to each word as if he saw them spelled out on a marquee.

"I can picture it. Can you?"

"It wouldn't be that hard to do. Not a lot of start-up costs, for one—I have most of the tools and equipment already, and I can use Pat's when I'm working with her. Of course, if I quit the dealership, we won't have my salary for a while. Or benefits. Pat said she has a bunch of work going a year out, though, and can keep me busy. And I'd want to get my own clients too, but I can wait on that."

"Well, we're set on our health insurance from the school district, so we're all good there."

"That's right."

"You have thought this through, Jim. I haven't heard you this excited since…for a really long time. So what's stopping us?"

"Us? So you're in?"

"All in, Jim. Truly. If you don't do it now, when are you going to? Pretty soon you'll be too old to lift a hammer."

"We use nail guns now."

"Aren't those even heavier?"

"Yes, they are," he said, imagining driving to that first job in a truck with the name of *his* company on the door. "I'll need a new work truck. That'll cost something up front."

"I knew this would end up with you getting a new truck somehow. Boys and their toys. Too bad you don't know a place you can get one of those."

"I'll turn in the SUV."

"The heck you will. I'll take the SUV. We can turn in my old Corolla."

"Deal."

JANELLE

Three weeks in and the program was looking up for Janelle. She had never felt more fulfilled. She was at an elite conservatory, playing the violin daily, writing music, and training with some of the best faculty and musicians in the country. She was even enjoying her part-time job at the café. It gave her mind a rest, and the extra money helped her to do what she loved most: playing the violin.

Janelle had grown up with many interests, and she took advantage of her liberal arts education to do as many of them as she could: music, soccer, reading, volunteering—whatever she could think of. That variety had been a great experience, and she loved it, but she loved this program too—how stimulating it was to focus intensely on her one great passion. That was how you became an expert, right? She wasn't a standout in the program, not yet, but after her jitters at the beginning of the term, she now felt more confident that she could—that she would—achieve her dream of becoming a concert violinist.

With these good feelings abounding, Janelle walked into that morning's class with confidence. Jazz Ensemble. Janelle had taken a liking to Professor Muñoz's class. Oscar Peterson, Art Blakey, Miles Davis, Sarah Vaughn, and the rest weren't her standard fare, but she had come to appreciate the virtuosity of jazz performers and composers alike. Thelonious Monk was a favorite composer, Ella Fitzgerald a favorite performer. There wasn't a huge history of jazz violin, but some of the early swing bands had string sections, and Professor Muñoz had directed her to the work of Jean-Luc Ponty in the 1960s. He had played with Elton John, who had his own section in her father's music collection, and with other pop stars. But she admired Ponty anyway. There was so much to learn.

Janelle plopped into her usual spot in the first row and to the right. "Hi, Padme," she said to the violinist who often sat next to her. Janelle didn't know why. Padme hadn't grown any friendlier since the first day, at least to Janelle. She stuck to the people she had known before the program.

True to form, Padme nodded acknowledgment, then returned to whatever she was viewing on her phone.

Determined not to lose her good mood, Janelle pulled out her notebook and arranged her sheet music while humming the Duke Ellington composition they had been assigned for that day. Professor Muñoz walked in. "Phones away." This was her signature greeting. Then she added something new. "Music away too. You won't be needing it. Today we're going to do something different. Well, not different for jazz. Normal for jazz. Improvisation. Jazz is all about improvisation."

Janelle's stomach turned. Improvisation? What about all the practice she had put in that week? She had been up until two in the morning most nights.

"I thought Ellington was today," Janelle whispered to Padme.

"Things change," Padme said without inflection. "Improvisation."

This was as close to a joke as Padme came, but it didn't help Janelle, her great mood swept away in a river of stomach acid.

"This'll give you a taste of the jazz improvisation class most of you will take next semester," Professor Muñoz continued. "And besides, I was getting bored. Instruments ready. Now, a good jazz musician can improvise on anything. We'll do 'Twinkle, Twinkle, Little Star.'" She pointed to the dark-haired clarinetist in the back row. "Renaldo. Give us the basic melody, then we'll go from there. You will each solo. On my cue." She twirled her index finger, and Renaldo played the first notes of the nursery song.

Janelle shook her head as she picked up her bow. She was not ready for this. She watched her classmates as they responded to the professor's prompt. They each had such interesting approaches depending on their instrument. Some added a touch of swing, others of bebop or fusion; some chose the cooler West Coast style, others hot jazz. There were a few rough patches, but in general they all played well, as if they had rehearsed. Padme played like silk. Dionne's fingers danced on the keyboards. Was everyone in on something she wasn't? As she watched other students take their turns, she fell into a state that was half reverie, half panic. In her head she worked through all the styles they had been studying in the class but couldn't decide on the right one for herself. The music seemed to stop, and she realized Professor Muñoz was pointing at her. Janelle scraped the bow across the strings, emitting a screech she hadn't heard since the ninth grade, then froze, running through the menu of styles again. She couldn't pick one, couldn't proceed without the music in front of her.

"I see that mind working," Professor Muñoz encouraged. "But it's the heart that counts in jazz. Go for it. Just play what you feel."

Janelle tried, but she couldn't. It was as if the music had been stoppered somewhere deep inside her and she couldn't squeeze it out.

When she saw that Janelle was truly stuck, the professor took pity and moved on.

Janelle stewed in shame until the last musician finished the exercise. Then she bolted out of class with her violin and bow in hand, forgetting her jacket and everything else.

Janelle collapsed on a bench in the quad, her instrument in her lap. The fall air was cooling, and in the shade of the artfully arranged trees, she shivered with the chill. Her tears felt icy on her cheeks. What a disaster! She had let her professor down. She had let the class down. But most of all she had let herself down. She knew what her passion was, but would she ever be good enough? Was she grasping it too tightly? Loving it so much she couldn't let go enough to be successful? Would it ever come as easily to her as it did to everybody else? Could she really do this? The hamster wheel was spinning away in her head.

Janelle jumped when Dionne plopped down beside her, holding Janelle's violin case. "Hey, roomie. Serenading the squirrels?" When Janelle didn't answer, she went on. "I waited a bit after class for you to come back, but I figured you'd at least want to protect that fine instrument of yours."

"Or throw it in the trees," Janelle said, sounding like a five-year-old even to herself.

"Now why would you do something like that over such a little blip?"

"Little blip? You were there. That couldn't have gone worse."

"Sure it could have. It could have been like those dreams where you're not wearing your—"

"But it wasn't a dream. It was real, and it was real bad."

"Did I ever tell you about the first time I had to sing and play in front of an audience? With my band, I mean."

"No," Janelle said.

"There I am, all high haired and made up—you've seen the pictures."

Janelle nodded.

"We're doing this intro, I don't even remember the song. I'm doing a little solo on the keyboards, then I play rhythm along with the drummer and the bassist so the lead guitarist can do *his* introduction, and I'm watching him for the cue to start singing—you know, 'cause it's my song—and I'm hunching over the keyboards, all hyped up because this is the first song of my first gig. I'm watching the guitarist, and I finally get the cue, and I swing my head to sing and smack the microphone right out of the stand with my forehead. I turn back to the guitarist, whose eyes go big, but he's on the ball enough to move into a different song so I can duck under the keyboard to replace the mike."

"That doesn't sound too bad."

"Oh, I'm not done. I did replace the mic, but when I went to sing backup, the mic was still dead, and no matter what I did, it wouldn't come back. I'm singing into a dead mike the rest of the show, and of course we had to dump all my songs. And to top it off, I had this huge red welt growing on my forehead. My bandmates never let me live it down."

"But you kept playing."

"What else was I going to do? There was nothing wrong with my keyboards."

"You're right." She took the case from her friend, laid the violin inside, unstrung the bow, snapped the case shut, and hurried away. Over her shoulder, she yelled, "Thanks, Dionne. You're the best."

"What'd I do?" Dionne called back.

"You kept playing."

*

"Back for your things?" Professor Muñoz asked when Janelle powered into the classroom. "Good. I was just about to lock up." The professor stood near the piano, rearranging the books of music that had been knocked askew during class.

"Can I play it now? I'm ready."

"You're ready? Now? I'm not sure you understand the definition of 'improvisation,' my dear," Professor Muñoz said, but not unkindly. "Don't worry. You'll get another chance."

"Please? Now?" Janelle snapped open her case, pulled out the violin, restrung her bow, and held the instrument ready. "I have to." She nodded at the piano.

Professor Muñoz held Janelle's eyes for a few beats, then leaned over and plunked out the introduction to "Twinkle, Twinkle." When she stopped, Janelle took it from there.

Janelle had planned it all out in her head as she sat on the bench, but now she couldn't remember a thing. She laughed to herself—there she was, overplanning again. As she was thinking all this, the bow started moving, her fingers took on a mind of their own, and soon she was traveling along with the notes as if they were the car of a roller coaster pulling her along. She forgot where she was and what she was doing and who was in the room and she simply played…until she heard clapping from a distance and saw Professor Muñoz next to the piano, smiling. Janelle dropped her bow hand, then lowered the violin itself, breathing hard as if she had actually been on a roller coaster.

"You made your point, my dear. Janelle, right?"

Janelle nodded, still not quite sure what she had just done.

"I think you got it there, in the second half. You let the music carry you away. That's improvisation. Improvisation is *fun*. Improvisation is *joy*. Improvisation is *passion*. Sometimes you can squeeze the joy out of passion. Passion isn't about squeezing, it's about letting go."

Janelle nodded.

"I'm guessing that didn't come easy to you."

Janelle shook her head.

"Yeah, I can see that about you. Remember how that feels." She walked toward her desk, then spun back toward Janelle. "Do you have anywhere else to be in the next few minutes?"

Janelle shook her head again. She was having trouble finding her words, stunned by the passion she had let loose in her own music.

"Then let's chat." Professor Muñoz pulled out one of the student chairs, turned it to face Janelle, and indicated Janelle do the same with the chair nearest her.

Reflection and Activity

Louis has had a passion for his family and his work for many years, but now that he is facing retirement, he is not sure what's ahead. It is only when he encounters the passion of young Qasim that he discovers how he might redirect his own. Jim has always known that his passion is working with his hands, especially in wood. He must learn to give himself the permission to pursue that dream instead of living a life of obligation and duty. Is Janelle squeezing her passion for music too hard? Professor Muñoz counsels Janelle that you can extinguish the joy from your passion if you don't learn to let go.

What is your passion? What do you love to do? What ignites your energy and brings you joy? When you lose all track of time, what are you likely to be doing? If you were granted an extra hour today, how would you spend it?

Take the next five to ten minutes and write down everything you can think of that you feel passionate about, that gives you joy. If you're drawing a blank, think back to the time/money activity from the values chapter. Where you spend your time and what you spend your money on can also point to what you're passionate about. What do you spend time doing? What do you think about when you have the time and space to daydream? On the other hand, if you look at what you spend your time and money on and say to yourself, *These are not my passions; these are not things I should be spending my energy on,* then you've gained self-awareness to correct your course. What *are* your true passions? How can you arrange to spend more time on them? What passions are serving you? What are not?

When you finish with your initial list, categorize your passions, and then ask yourself a few questions. Are you passionate only about what you're good at? Do you shy away from opportunities because you don't think you excel at them, because you don't want to risk failure? Your next great passion may be just around the corner if you have the courage and gumption to go after it.

On the other hand, are some of what you think of as passions more along the lines of time killers or obsessions? Internet surfing? Social media? Video gaming? Gardening? All of these activities done in moderation can be fun, genuine passions. But when taken to a negative extreme—and I think we all know how that feels—they can become more like addictions that give us the opposite of joy, that make us feel bad about ourselves, that eat away at our happiness instead of nurturing it, that disconnect us from our relationships. The kind of passions we're talking about in *Grab the Helm* are positive forces, forces for the good, that drive us toward the true purpose that defines our life.

To help you visualize the two sides of the coin, let's take another look at the four color energies:

Red energy: Those who lead with Red are more apt to have a passion for making decisions, completing tasks, and moving things forward. But sometimes when they are so focused on checking the boxes, they don't slow down enough to see the impact of their actions and decisions on others.

Yellow energy: Those who lead with Yellow are more apt to have a passion for inspiring others, for connecting and networking. But they can get so caught up in the big picture they lose sight of important details and aren't able to get things done.

Green energy: Those who lead with Green are more apt to have a passion for building trust and forming close relationships, for giving and receiving support. If they feel their trust has been betrayed, however, they can give in to negative emotions and lash out in a passive-aggressive way.

Blue energy: Those who lead with Blue are more apt to be passionate about analyzing details, collecting data, examining every possible scenario. In this way, they hope to reduce risk. But in doing so, they may become lost in the weeds of details and become paralyzed and incapable of moving forward.

Each color is driven by specific passions and encompasses both positive and negative energies. Leading from the Helm requires balance, and this is particularly true of passion. We should live our passions in balance and moderation so that they don't push us toward obsession on the one hand and drudgery on the other. We all have to do things we are not particularly passionate about. That is part of life. You may not be fueled by balancing the books of your company or household, or writing that essay for the history class you must take to fulfill general requirements, but completing these tasks clears the way for engaging in your true passions.

Or maybe you engage your passions first to revive your energy so you can face these other tasks and duties in a good frame of mind. Jumping on your bike, doing yoga, brainstorming with a coworker, or spending time with your kids before you tackle these tasks may be just what you need to clear your head in order to get stuff done. It's about managing your fuel supply to refuel your fire. Passion is both a means of refueling your fire and the fire itself.

Considering this discussion of passion, return to your list. Are you using your passions to refuel? What passions are not as important as they used to be? What passions do you want to spend more time and energy on? How can you make more time for these passions? Be specific. Use your calendar. Record right now the time and date you are going to engage in one of the passions on your list.

Go to www.grabthehelm.com to enter your reflections and access more information.

CHAPTER 6

THE SIXTH SPOKE OF THE HELM
TALENT

Hide not your talents, they for use were made.
What's a sundial in the shade?

—Benjamin Franklin

W e spend a lifetime learning, understanding, and developing our talents—a process of trial and error to figure out what we are really good at. In this way, we all have a tool chest of talents, gifts, skills, and knowledge, and these are often linked to our passions—it's much easier to be passionate about something we have a talent for. Sometimes, however, we don't see the full range and potential of what we can do. Are you aware of all of the gifts you possess?

Talent has two faces. On the one, your talents are the natural gifts you're given at birth, your aptitudes, your abilities—facility with numbers or languages, IQ, a high vertical leap, hand-eye coordination, an ear for music, and so on. On the other, talent is what you learn over a lifetime, the knowledge, abilities, and expertise you teach yourself or learn from others. The two are intertwined. If you don't nurture your natural talents, they will wither away. And if you're not pushing to learn new talents and skills, you can't really uncover all of what you are capable of doing. If you're not growing, you're dying.

So how *are* you using your gifts? I firmly believe we have an obligation and a choice to use our talents—an obligation to ourselves and to the community at large. When we build our individual talents, we work to our strengths. We feel good about ourselves because we are good at something. The more competent we feel, the more confident we feel, and this gives us the strength and courage to go after opportunities. We are a social species, and if we have the ability, the talent, to raise up the community, to serve others, then we should take the opportunity to do so.

Sometimes we shy away from sharing our gifts out of complacency or fear. Maybe we're scared of taking a risk, of failing at something we're supposed to be good at. We don't want to find out that we're not so good after all. Maybe we think the way things are is "good enough." We don't want to rock the boat, because we might fall in the water. But how will we know all we are capable of doing if we're afraid of getting wet? If we don't push ourselves to grow, to continue forward, these hidden gifts will never be revealed.

To live a life full of purpose, it's important to recognize our talents by practicing self-awareness, by showing gratitude for the gifts we recognize, and by developing the tool chest of gifts that align with who we are and who we want to be. We are stewards of our gifts. Exercise the genius inside you.

LOUIS

Yes, Qasim was very… energetic, as Louis's team had suggested. But after working with him for almost three weeks, Louis found himself taken with a young man who had so much confidence and passion. And his talent was out of sight.

Louis had prided himself on staying up to date with all the financial tools available for a company their size, but Qasim was a true wizard. He had been able to go back to the original databases and run some analytic tools he had learned in school to create a range of forecasts for many possible scenarios for the company, from no-growth to high-growth and everything in between, taking into account different economic models for the region, for the country, and for the global marketplace.

Not that Louis couldn't have done this on his own, but it would have taken a lot longer, and the result wouldn't have been anywhere near as effective and impressive. Using his media design skills, Qasim had changed an old-fashioned white paper—the kind that went from inboxes to file drawers after the thumbing of a few pages—to a multimedia extravaganza with animations and embedded video. All they needed was James Earl Jones to read Louis's parts and they'd be all set.

"No, no, you'll sound great recorded, just like that speech at Harvey," Qasim had assured him. Qasim helped Louis use the corner office studio for the first time. After getting used to speaking into a microphone in a booth by himself rather than in front of a responsive audience, Louis laid down the narration tracks after two or three takes, with Qasim as the sound engineer. When Qasim said, "All right, I'll just do the editing and we'll be finished," Louis had insisted that Qasim teach him how to edit both the video and sound files, though he saw the wisdom in having Qasim produce the final cut, which they had just reviewed that day, the day of Louis's "surprise" party.

"That's good work, Qasim. I've been reading about how the world is moving to more visual communication, and I think I finally have a sense of what that means."

"You're a quick learner, Louis. And I'm not BSing you. You have a presence—the way you hold yourself, the way you speak. You're really good at this. You could run for office or something."

"That's very flattering, Qasim, but I'm retiring for a reason, though it's been great working with you. I almost wish I weren't retiring so we could continue to work together. *Almost.*"

"You know, Louis, I've been thinking about that, and I have a few ideas."

This guy has no fear, Louis thought.

"Remember what I told you about how I had to scramble for scholarships when I was putting myself through college?"

Louis nodded.

"I was thinking of forming a foundation to do that. To provide fellowships to people like me—and you, when you were younger."

"A foundation. That's ambitious of you. But aren't you putting the cart before the horse? Don't you set up a foundation after you've made it big?"

"I can't wait that long. There's a need for it now, and if we get the right people involved…I've done some research. Setting up the foundation isn't the hard part—you just have to sign a lot of papers and pay some fees. No, the hard part is raising the money, then giving it away to worthy candidates. Most foundations fail because they're run by people with good hearts who don't really know finance. So the foundation needs someone who knows finance and is a great spokesperson as well. Do you know anyone like that? Maybe someone with some time on his hands?"

"Qasim, are you offering me a job?"

"Ye-es?" Qasim sounded tentative for the first time in their brief acquaintance.

Louis was running through the possibilities in his head, and the more he thought about it, the more he liked the idea. "You make a good case, but I can do you one better. My wife and I have been looking for something like this for a while. We might be willing to provide some seed money, an initial donation. Now, she's also an attorney, so I'd want her to look everything over before we sign anything—for you too."

"I can't afford an attorney right now."

"Don't worry about that." Louis waved him off.

"Really?" Qasim was so excited he was practically jumping in place. "You'd consider doing this?"

"Absolutely. You're a world changer, Qasim, and I'm not so old I don't want to be part of that. How many other kids out there have your kind of talent and won't have the chance to develop it?" Louis looked at his watch, then put his hand on Qasim's shoulder. "Isn't it time to find some excuse to take me to your desk so we can get the surprise party underway?"

"You know about that? Okay, then, I have something to show you at my desk." He indicated the door with a flourish.

Louis gestured that Qasim should go first, which he did, with Louis following behind, thinking not of the impending party but of how he could adapt the processes he had built for the company to a not-for-profit foundation. This was something he had had the skills and knowledge to get behind.

*

Once Louis and Qasim arrived at Qasim's desk in the bullpen, everyone on the floor jumped out from wherever they were hiding and yelled, "Surprise!" The cheer was so loud, Louis jumped as if he actually had been surprised.

Rebecca was the emcee, with Manuel, the CEO, standing beside her. "Louis, you have been a stalwart of this firm for many years, during which you were instrumental in taking us from a three-person pop-up to our current configuration of two-hundred-plus in five different offices. Without your firm hand at the helm of our finance department and your analytic prowess, we might all be working as baristas. So, let me present to you, as a token of our appreciation for your work and leadership decade after decade...a card and a cupcake."

She signaled to someone outside the exit doors, which swung open slowly. Two team members marched in holding a banner-sized envelope between them, addressed to Louis. Trailing in their wake was another team member pushing a cart, and on the cart was a chocolate cupcake the size of a wedding cake.

Louis laughed out loud.

"And that, ladies and gentlemen, is a gotcha. We finally gotcha, Louis, but we wish we could have you another forty-five years." With that, tears welled in Rebecca's eyes until Louis rescued her with a hug and whispered, "Thank you."

Louis shook Manuel's hand, then shook and hugged his way around the room. His thank-you speech was as short and sweet as one of his meetings. "Thank you all. It's been my honor and privilege to work with all of you. Truly. I'm not thinking of this as the end, but as the beginning of the next adventure, where I'll apply old talents, as limited as they might be, to new challenges, and where this old dog may even learn a few new tricks." In the midst of the enthusiastic applause, Louis nodded to Qasim, who had his hands in his pockets and was rocking front to back on the balls of his feet.

JIM

On his drive home that night, the more Jim thought about "Bulldog Fine Home Remodeling," the more excited he became. This could be the great new chapter in his life that used *all* his gifts. The car dealership had been good to him, he knew that, and he was grateful. It had required many of his talents: customer service, finance, drive, organization, and leadership, but it had run its course. Running his own remodeling business would require all that as well as his skills in woodworking and design—the whole package. He had always believed if you had a talent you owed it to yourself—and the world—to use it. And this whole time he hadn't realized he wasn't living his own beliefs. Not that he had been lying to himself, exactly, but his drive to take care of his family, though not a bad thing by any means, had blinded him to some of his other strengths.

Could he go on as he was, working ten, fifteen more years at the lot and doing woodworking in his free time? Sure, he could try. But first, as GM he had very little free time as it was, and he didn't see that changing. And second, now that he had gotten the taste in the last few weeks of building things full time, he wasn't sure he could go back to doing it a couple of hours on the weekends. This wasn't a midlife crisis; it was more of a midlife correction. If this was how Dionne felt about her music, then he owed her a huge apology.

When he pulled into the driveway, he turned off the radio and called his daughter. Based on what he remembered of her schedule, he didn't think she'd be in class.

"Dad?" Dionne answered. "What's wrong? Is Mom all right? It's not Sunday."

"Whoa, everything's fine. I just wanted to talk. A father can't call his daughter more than once a week?"

"You never have before."

"Fair enough. Nothing's wrong. How's school?" While he talked, he absentmindedly played with the button that locked and unlocked the car doors.

"Going well, actually. I mean, it's hard, but I'm learning a lot. Don't worry, I think I'm really getting what I'm paying for."

Dionne seemed to be walking while she talked, the ambient noise making it a little hard to hear everything she said. Jim spoke louder to compensate. "That's what I wanted to talk about. I've been doing a lot of remodeling lately."

"You do make the best tree houses in town, that's for sure."

"More than that. I took some time off to work on a project for Pat."

"Mom told me."

"Did Mom also tell you that I love it? It's amazing how quick the time goes by when you work on something you love, especially something you're good at." He stopped playing with the locks. "Just like you and your music. I get it now. You're such a great musician, so talented. You really blew all the other musicians out of the water in high school. I loved bragging that you were my daughter."

"Thanks, Dad. It was a little embarrassing, but in the end it made me feel good."

"It'd be a shame to let all that skill go to waste."

"Dad, that's what—"

"I know, I know, that's what I'm trying to tell you. I *agree* with you. And I'm so proud of you sticking to your guns. You knew what you wanted and you went for it. Not everyone would have had the guts to stand up to their old man like you did. I'm sorry I came down on you so hard. Doing what I'm doing now, I see how rewarding it is to do what you're good at, what you care about, and what makes you happy." Jim paused before continuing. "I guess I learned a thing or two from you. I'm quitting the dealership."

"What? I thought I'd never hear those words out of your mouth."

"And starting up my own remodeling business."

"Oh, Dad, that's so cool! Wait. Does Mom know?"

"Of course she does. It was partly her idea."

"Okay, good. Then I can really say, 'Oh, Dad, that's so cool.' And it is. I'm proud of you. This is really good."

"I'm proud of you too, honey. More proud than you will ever know." He sniffed.

"Dad. Are you tearing up?"

"What? No. My eyes are a little itchy from the dust at the work site. Now don't you have some practicing to do? Don't let that skill get rusty." He waited until he hung up to wipe the tears from his cheeks with his newly calloused fingers.

JANELLE

Once Professor Muñoz and Janelle settled into the chairs facing each other, the professor spoke. "I'm a musician, you know, so I've learned how to read a room over the years, and a classroom is no different. I've been watching you from the beginning, Miss Janelle."

"You have?"

"Yes, I have."

"I am so sorry I froze up like that and ran out of class. It'll never happen again. I don't know what got into me. I usually come through in the clutch." Janelle grabbed the sides of the desk and hung on as if it were a steering wheel.

Professor Muñoz waved her hand. "I'm not worried about that. You're not the first to freeze in improv, and you won't be the last. I'm surprised more folks didn't freeze up today. This is a very talented group."

"Aren't they, though? I wish I had that kind of talent, but I know I don't. That's why I work so hard. I just want this so bad, and I feel like no matter how hard I work, I'm always behind. If that's not the cruelty of the universe, I don't know what is."

"Of course you have talent," Professor Muñoz said. "Substantial talent. You wouldn't be here if you didn't. The truth is, everyone here's got talent, and if you could measure these things, which sometimes I doubt, it would be safe to say that some members of the program have more musical skill than you, and some have less. It's what you do with it that counts. And the fact that you started later…that just makes you all the more driven."

"How'd you know that?"

"I read your application—all three times. You're very persistent."

She opened her hand toward her red tote, where Janelle assumed she kept her files.

"Thank you."

"Don't thank me yet. I have a question for you."

"Okay."

"Are you having fun?"

"Fun? Yeah, of course. This is my dream."

"That's not what I asked. Are you having fun? Because the woman in those applications who did all those different things like soccer and volunteering and whatever else seemed to be having more fun than the woman in front of me."

"I just want to be the best."

"But I don't want you to focus on being the best."

Janelle pushed herself up straight. "What? Aren't we all supposed to try to be the best?"

"To try your best, yes, of course, but that's different. Always trying to be *the* best, that can be—limiting, really. I know that sounds counterintuitive, but think about it. If you're always trying to be the best, you're always comparing yourself to others. You're not worried about developing your own talent. You're worried about other people."

"I never thought of it that way."

"Look, Janelle." Professor Muñoz leaned forward to emphasize her point.

Janelle took her hands from the sides of her desk, folded them in her lap, leaned away from the professor.

"I've taught a lot of students, most of whom have been brilliant musicians like yourself. You have so much time left in this program. You can't beat yourself up about a tiny setback."

Janelle furrowed her brow, trying to understand. "You're telling me to stop trying so hard?"

"Not exactly," Professor Muñoz said, leaning back. "There are different ways to nurture talent. You have something a lot of the kids in the program don't have. Perspective and a late-bloomer's passion. Doing only one thing for your whole life can really beat it out of you. You're a talented violinist, but you still love playing. A lot of those kids don't anymore. Trust me, the fact that you've been able to do other things is a plus for you."

"How? I want a career in music. How am I possibly going to compete against all this other talent?"

"By not competing. Your life is more than just this program. You're well rounded—you have many gifts—and I'm a firm believer that all one's gifts come through in the music. This is one moment in your very large and rich life. Imagine your life as a wheel—everything must stay in balance or the wheel will spin out of control."

"I hear you, I do," Janelle said carefully. "But I'm not going to back off. Music is my passion and dream, and there are certain expectations to fulfill."

"Sometimes expectations turn into boundaries," Professor Muñoz said. "Our own and others'."

Professor Muñoz watched Janelle ponder this.

"Please be kind to yourself," she went on. "I want you to lead a life with unapologetic purpose, and with a greater understanding of yourself. You're in a place where your passions and talents align—you're very fortunate to have this kind of an opportunity. But this is still a time of huge transformation. Stay curious and open."

Janelle nodded.

"We have to allow ourselves and others the time, patience, and space to grow into who we really are."

Janelle thought of Padme.

As if Professor Muñoz could read her mind, she added, "And give others the space to do so as well."

Janelle took a moment to take everything in. She looked directly at her professor. "You know I'm going to continue to work just as hard, right?"

"I'm glad you're listening," Professor Muñoz said, smiling. "Of course I expect nothing less. I want you to make your mark here. But I also want you to find the courage to nurture and develop all your talents, to experiment and experience all those things that speak to your soul. I know there is more in your soul than music, but it's all tied together. Develop all your gifts, then whenever you can, use them to make the world a better place."

"Do you really think I can?"

"I know you can."

"Thank you, Professor," Janelle said.

"At the end of the day, you are the author of your own life. Don't let someone else write your story. Don't cut yourself off from the other things that give you joy. What do you normally do when you need a break? What helps?"

"That's easy. I used to go out and play soccer. Or at least kick the ball around if it was just me."

"Used to?"

"I stopped that when I came here. I don't want to be distracted."

"Distracted is just what you need to be. We all do every once in a while. Go do your soccer, and if you can find someone else to do it with you, all the better."

Janelle smiled for the first time since the improv disaster. "Homework. I can do that."

Reflection and Activity

With the help of Qasim, Louis is developing an untapped talent for public speaking and is mulling over how to apply the skills he learned in the business world to the world of nonprofit foundations. Jim realizes more strongly what he has suspected all along, that he hasn't been using all his natural and developed gifts. In a phone conversation, he apologizes to Dionne and gives her credit for doing what she had to to nurture her talent in music. Professor Muñoz reminds Janelle that she has many skills in addition to music, and she does herself and the community no favors by letting them wither.

What are your talents—the natural gifts you were born with and the skills you acquired through perseverance and hard work?

In this exercise, list all your talents, skills, abilities, and expertise you can think of. Are you particularly fast? Do you have good hand-eye coordination? Do you have a natural ability to pick up instruments or languages? Maybe French class wasn't easy for you, but you worked at the language until now you can understand French films without subtitles. Did you work really hard to make the baseball team? Have you seen progress in your sketchbook? Are you good with numbers? Are you good at teaching, at organizing events, at persuasion, at writing, at public speaking? Include the things you have a natural gift for as well as those you've picked up over the years. List everything you can think of. Don't be shy, and don't sell yourself short.

If you're comfortable with the idea, to expand the list, ask trusted friends or family to weigh in on your talents, and add the new ones. Don't prompt them! They may point to things you don't recognize in yourself or don't give yourself credit for.

Remember, too, that talents can change over the years. Physical talents can be short-lived, for example. Maybe you were the fastest kid on the track team in junior high, and now, with age, all you can manage is a little jogging for exercise. Eyesight worsens, reflexes slow down, bones grow more brittle. At the same time, though, we develop new skills. We learn better self-control, we achieve greater wisdom, we learn to communicate better with a greater range of people, we finally put our mind to learning another language to go with our appetite for travel.

Add to your list any of these recently developed talents you might have left out.

Now take a closer look at the items on your list. Are you actively using all your talents? Practicing and nurturing them? Do you share your gifts with others, either by teaching or by applying them in ways that benefit others? If you are particularly good at digital photography, for example, do you help others with tips and techniques? If you are a good fundraiser, have you offered your services to a worthy community group that needs help raising money?

It takes courage to share your talents. You must be willing to make mistakes and embrace fear, to experience new things and explore outside your comfort zone. I sure was terrified sailing in the North Atlantic during that storm I told you about in the preface. But Dave and I chose to face down our fear and turned to the knowledge and skills we had and used the frightening opportunity to learn new ones. That experience sharpened my sailing abilities, and every time I'm out on the water, I learn more.

Are there opportunities in your life to use your talents that you're not taking advantage of? Do you rationalize that you don't *really* have the skill to do such and such, even though you always wanted to try? Now is the time to step through that door of opportunity, which we'll talk about in the next chapter. You have more talent than you think, and by using those skills, you can achieve much more than you ever thought possible.

Just as living with purpose is a daily journey of discovery, so is leveraging our talents. To make our skills and knowledge most useful to ourselves and others, we must cultivate them with wisdom and courage, share them, and align them with all the other spokes of the helm. If passion is the foundation of Leading from the Helm, as I suggested in the previous chapter, then talent provides the tools we use to build on that foundation. Go forth and share your gifts with the world, whether these gifts are natural born or hard won. Both you and the world will be the better off.

Go to www.grabthehelm.com to enter your reflections and access more information.

CHAPTER 7

THE SEVENTH SPOKE OF THE HELM
OPPORTUNITY

How much I missed simply because
I was afraid of missing it.
—Paulo Coelho

Every day, life opens many doors of opportunity for us to step through. And every day, life gives us a choice. Do we walk through the door, pass on by, or miss it altogether?

The door may be an opportunity for learning, for advancing your career, for meeting someone you've always admired, for service to others, for self-reflection, for investing in yourself with time, effort, or money, for connecting with someone new. There are an untold number of opportunities depending on your circumstances and who you are. But none of them mean a thing if you don't have the courage and strength to say yes to these opportunities, a courage and strength that comes at least in part from faith in yourself to step into the unknown. To take advantage of the opportunities life has to offer, you must be intentional, purposeful, mindful, and present. Without these qualities, you may not see all the opportunities right in front of you.

It's not always easy to boldly walk through the door. We tend to live in the past, worry about the future, and fear the unknown on the other side. We come up with a thousand reasons why we can't or shouldn't step through. Sometimes we dismiss the opportunity too quickly; other times we take too long to think about it. Either way we lose out. We are fearful and apprehensive, and when we pass up an opportunity by giving in to these fears, we deny ourselves the virtually unlimited possibilities for growth in our lives. Doors won't stay open forever.

At the same time, we always have a choice. Sometimes it is better not to pursue an opportunity if the negative impact outweighs the positive. The point is, we should not shy away simply because of our insecurities.

When we are present and mindful, we open ourselves to vast opportunities. Sometimes we happen upon an opportunity; sometimes we seek out our own opportunities; and sometimes others show them to us. No matter what, it is important to allow ourselves the chance to take a new opportunity, to correct our course. If we program the GPS, set the engine, and worry only about getting to the destination, we won't be prepared to shift course if a better one arises. The best opportunities often come to us when we are in the right place at the right time with the right mindset.

To take advantage of the opportunities we encounter, I suggest using a model we call the Four A's:

- Awareness
- Appreciation
- Accountability
- Action

Awareness is the start, the awakening. We acknowledge the opportunity before us, and we are now alive to its possibilities, whether we have created it ourselves, someone has created it for us, or we've simply happened upon it. The next step is appreciating the opportunity, seeing it truly, as it is, now, in front of us. Do we understand all the implications of the opportunity? Is it a good opportunity, despite the potential risks, perhaps even a great opportunity? If we truly appreciate everything the opportunity offers, we are more likely to take the next two steps. That's when we ask ourselves the question: In taking this opportunity, are we accountable to our values, passions, and purpose? If the answer is yes, then we take action.

Our goal in this book is to help you discover your purpose. You will never know your true purpose without accepting the opportunities to experience all of what life has to offer. Saying yes to opportunity can be difficult—gut-wrenching, even. It may take a great deal of courage and effort. If you are willing to step into these moments, however, I promise you will have a profound impact on your life and the lives of others—and perhaps even the world at large.

Be fearless, be mindful, chart your course, and remember that every moment is an opportunity.

JANELLE

After her talk with Professor Muñoz, Janelle went straight back to her room instead of to the rehearsal space as she usually would have done. Professor Muñoz was right. What was wrong with taking a break and getting some exercise?

Once in the apartment, Janelle dumped her backpack and violin case on the bed, grabbed a protein bar from her stash, and dug through her dresser for her old practice gear, which she had hidden away for reasons she now didn't really understand. She dressed, then found the deflated soccer ball in the corner of the closet and spent another five minutes searching for a hand pump, which she found in a desk drawer. Once she pumped up the ball, she put her keys and ID on a wrist lanyard, grabbed her water bottle, and headed out to the quad, wearing sneakers instead of spikes. She didn't want to tear up the manicured lawn.

On the quad were the usual array of people tossing around Frisbees or footballs with varying degrees of skill and enthusiasm, as well as afternoon nappers disguised as students at their studies. Janelle jogged to an empty part of the lawn, propped her things up against one of the trees, stretched, then threw the soccer ball out on the lawn and ran after it. When she caught up to it, she trapped it, then dribbled in a circle, tapping the ball with each foot, reversing field, doing the kinds of ball-handling drills she could do by herself: juggling the ball with her knees and feet and head, crossover dribbles, pushing the ball ahead and chasing it down. She was a little rusty, and it would take her more than fifteen minutes to get her soccer legs back, but she soon lost herself in the effort, forgetting everything but the ball, the grass, and her pumping heart. Why had she thought she was past this again?

She worked it for a few more minutes, then stopped for a breath, standing tall, her hands on her hips. That's when she heard someone clapping—the second time that day, she realized—and looked over to the tree where she had left her gear. There was Dionne sitting on the grass in leggings and a tunic.

"Hey, you're pretty good," Dionne called out.

"Did you think I was lying?" Janelle dribbled the ball Dionne's way.

"Now I see it with my own eyes."

"You're pretty chipper," Janelle said, toeing the ball while they talked.

"I just got off the phone with my dad, and he said the strangest thing."

"What's that?"

"'I'm sorry.'"

Janelle laughed. "Is that so rare?"

"He never apologizes. And he said he's proud of me. I'm still in shock."

"That makes two of us. I talked with Professor Muñoz."

"How'd that go?"

"I did my improv for her, and she said I did well, so that was good. But then afterward she told me she didn't want me to try to be the best. That she wanted me to play the music and let my soul shine through or something. What teacher tells you not to try to be the best?"

"A smart one."

"I guess. She also told me to play more soccer and to get others to play with me...so up you go." She stretched out her hand.

"What, me? I'm more of a kickball kind of girl." But Dionne reached out and let Janelle pull her to her feet.

"Same idea, kind of, only you don't kick the ball with your toe, you kick and control it with the inside or outside of your foot. Like this." Janelle moved the ball between her feet while she backed up. "Here, you try it."

She tapped the ball toward Dionne who, despite the instructions, kicked at it with her toe, sending it skittering off to the side. Janelle sprinted after the ball to retrieve it and said, "Don't just kick it. Trap it first, like this." She put her foot on top of the ball. "Then pass it." She tapped it again toward Dionne, who let the ball hit her foot until it stopped. "That's it. Now pass it to me." Dionne's foot scraped the ground in front of the ball before she kicked it, but at least the ball squirted toward Janelle this time. "That's it. Watch your foot hit the ball."

They passed the ball back and forth, Janelle moving them farther apart each time. What Dionne lacked in skill she made up for in enthusiasm, smiling the whole time and giggling when she kicked it.

"Okay, let's step it up. Kick to me as hard as you can."

Dionne stepped back, ran at the ball, and kicked it as hard as she could—twenty yards to Janelle's left.

"Dionne! Look where you're kicking." Janelle pivoted to track down the ball but slowed when she saw that someone else had joined them. Dionne had known what she was doing all along. This someone had trapped the ball expertly and juggled it with the biggest smile on her face. She clearly knew what she was doing. Janelle stopped still when she saw who it was. Padme. Great, another thing she could lord over Janelle.

Padme trapped the ball, then zipped a sharp pass to Janelle. "You play soccer," she said without the bite Janelle expected.

Janelle didn't want to ruin her good mood, so she responded neutrally. "So do you."

"Of course. It's the only thing that keeps me sane—something that's not music." She passed the ball to Dionne. It bounced off Dionne's knee erratically.

"And I don't." Dionne laughed good naturedly. "Does that mean I'm insane?"

"If the cleats fit...or don't fit, in your case," Janelle teased.

Padme retrieved the ball and nailed another pass to Janelle.

"You know what you're doing, that's for sure," Janelle said.

"Not as good as you, though. I've been watching a few minutes. You *really* know what you're doing," Padme said with genuine admiration. "I was kind of middle of the pack. I bet you were captain."

Who was this new Padme? "We were a smallish school," Janelle said. "But yeah."

As they spoke, they tested each other with more difficult passes and ball handling, while Dionne retired to sit under the tree, content to watch. Padme lit up. She really did like soccer. They finally slowed a bit and drifted over to Dionne.

"Well, thanks for letting me join in. That's the most fun I've had since I got here," Padme said.

"What about your music?"

"Oh, sure, I like to play music, but in my family it's more of a duty than fun, really. The family business."

"I guess I didn't think of it that way. Yeah, I had fun too. How about you?" She toed the ball to Dionne, who swatted it away with her hand.

"Does that answer your question?"

All three laughed.

Janelle retrieved the ball, flipped it up in the air behind her, leaned backward, caught the ball on her forehead, and balanced it like a sea lion.

"That's so cool. I wish I was that good at something other than music."

"But you are," Janelle said.

"Not really," Padme responded modestly.

"I'd play with you any time."

"Do you mean it?"

"Yeah," Janelle said, wondering what Padme was getting at.

"We should join the tournament."

"What tournament?"

"It's coming up in a couple of weeks, after midterms. The grad schools compete against each other in different sports— softball, touch football, ultimate Frisbee, volleyball, soccer. I think we still have time to enter."

"I don't know, with midterms coming up…"

"Oh, c'mon, we all need a break. You already practice twice as much as the rest of us."

"Because I need to."

"Hardly."

Had Padme complimented her music? Janelle thought she must be dreaming.

"Now, soccer," Padme continued, businesslike. "I know a bunch of people who'd be interested. All we need is someone who really knows what they're doing. You know, like a captain. Know anybody like that?"

"Not really."

"Do I need to beg?"

"That I'd like to see."

Padme didn't laugh at the joke. "This is it. This is me begging. Are you in or not?"

"A method of begging with which I am not familiar."

Dionne jumped in. "She'll do it."

"What?" Janelle snapped.

"I'm her agent. She'll do it."

"All right, all right, but only if you're co-captain," Janelle said to Padme. "And you're doing it too." This to Dionne.

Padme nodded, pleased to be asked. "I can do that."

"I'll help out," Dionne said. "But I don't think I'll be playing much."

"We'll need *someone* to hand out the towels," Janelle said.

"We've created a monster," Dionne retorted.

"Let's go. Pizza on me," Padme said. "We've got a soccer team to put together."

LOUIS

Louis made his way from the garage through the mudroom into the kitchen. In one hand he carried a shopping bag emitting the aroma of their go-to Thai takeout, in the other a cake box with a generous portion of his retirement cupcake.

"Thai—yes, perfect," Madeline said, waving her hand in the air. "No one should be cooking today."

"Quite the dust cloud." Louis swung the bag onto the counter along with the box.

"Yeah, I think it was the sanding in the basement. It's coming along quite nicely, though. You should check it out. How was the party? What's in the box?"

"A portion of my retirement cupcake."

Madeline raised her eyebrows.

"At one point I had cracked to Rebecca that all I wanted for a party was a card and a cupcake, so of course they got me the biggest card and cupcake they could find. The card's still in the back seat. The cupcake is quite good, actually."

"Of course they did. You're going to miss them. Your second family."

"I will miss them terribly. But the most extraordinary thing happened today." He spoke while pulling the plastic carryout containers from the bags.

"You mean beside your retirement?" Madeline reached in for the napkins and chopsticks. "Congratulations, by the way. We should probably eat in the family room. Less dust there."

They carried their dinner into the family room. Madeline laid out napkins and chopsticks on their coffee table of golden oak. Louis set out the various containers and opened the lids.

"I was offered a job. By a twenty-five-year-old. And I think I took it!"

"Was that the young man helping you with the report?"

"Yes. What a bundle of energy and ideas." He explained Qasim's idea for the foundation. "So I guess I'd be the spokesperson/CFO, giving speeches, raising money, keeping track of the money. It's all still up in the air, but I've agreed on principle And I offered your services too, for the legal stuff. You don't mind, do you? We'll put you on the board."

"Lordy, another board. Your first day of retirement and you've already caught on to the most important skill in the not-for-profit world: how to 'volunteer' someone for a job."

"Is that why you're on so many boards?"

"I'm afraid so."

"Oh, and I sort of promised that we'd be the first donors, provide the seed money. So that's why I want to be part of it too. To make sure the money is used wisely."

"I'm sure it will be, with you at the helm. I've been meaning to get some of our money into a trust for a few years now. What an opportunity. This comes at a great time."

"That's what I was thinking. Why wait until we're gone for our legacy to kick in? This way we have a say about how it works."

Madeline slurped a rice noodle into her mouth, shook her head. "I figured you'd never fully retire, but I thought you'd give yourself a few weeks."

"Oh, I'm sure I'll be able to take it easy. It won't be like running a company."

Madeline laughed hard, so hard Louis thought she might be choking. He jumped up from the couch, but Madeline waved him away.

"What?" Louis said.

"You're right. It won't be like running a company—it'll be harder. But I still think we should do it. It'll be the perfect new career for you."

"I think I can still bring something to the table."

"Besides this great food?" She indicated the feast on the coffee table.

"Besides that."

"Oh, Louis, honey. I'm so excited. Seems like you were getting a little worried there about what came next. And here it is, just like that. Opportunity." She snapped her fingers.

"I'm going to work it at the other end too. If I could inspire Qasim with one brief talk, what could we do if it was more of a regular part of the curriculum? I'm going to give the dean a call, see if they could use something like that."

Madeline beamed at him, emotion welling up in her eyes. "What?"

"You've always been a good teacher."

"Me?"

"You've always had the gift. I hear you talking to the grandkids, always giving advice and help—good advice, mostly. And they listen to you. You coached the boys in baseball growing up. Even when you weren't their actual coach, I might add."

Louis grimaced.

"And you couldn't have done what you did at the firm without sharing your vision with the team. What is that other than teaching? And now you have the opportunity to pass on your knowledge to the next generations *and* put your money where your mouth is. I'm just so happy you finally figured it out."

"Thanks for the free consulting."

"Free? You're in charge of cleanup."

JIM

The crew had been with Jim in the morning, but he had been alone in the afternoon, doing more of the finish work on his own. Done for the day, he climbed the stairs to the kitchen, then stopped short when he saw Madeline and an older man he took to be her husband moving about. "Whoops—sorry," he said. "I stayed a little later today. I didn't mean to interrupt."

"You're fine, Jim," Madeline said. "We're just cleaning up. Jim, this is my husband, Louis." She put her arm through Louis's. "Louis, this is Jim, the genius behind the renovation.

Patricia really was right about you, you know," she said to Jim. "You really give it the personal touch."

Louis reached out his hand. "Wonderful to finally meet you."

"Likewise," Jim said.

"I can't tell you how much I've appreciated your efforts. We've been wanting to get the basement redone since the kids moved out."

"Twenty years ago," Madeline reminded him.

"Right. Anyway, I'm terrible with this kind of stuff. But it makes such a big difference, so I really appreciate you doing it. You like Thai?" He indicated the stacks of containers ready for the fridge.

"Love it, actually, but I have to say no, thanks. My turn to cook."

"A man who cooks," Madeline said, nudging Louis.

"Some things are better left to the experts."

"Hardly. I'm making this chicken pasta dish I learned from my mom. Nothing too complicated."

"Now that you're retired, my dear..." Madeline said.

"Retired? Congratulations," Jim said to Louis. "How long's it been?"

Louis looked at his watch. "About an hour and a half."

They all had a good laugh.

"Jim has a day job," Madeline said. "He's the GM at that Toyota dealership over by my salon. He took some time off for our basement, actually. When do you have to go back?"

"Monday," he said. "But only for a few weeks, until they can find a replacement. I've made a big decision. That is, my wife and I have made a big decision. I'm going to do this full time: Bulldog Fine Home Remodeling."

"What a great idea!" Madeline said. "You'll be perfect. Hey, you know, dear," she said to Louis. "Now that the basement is almost finished, it might be time to do the master suite. Let us know when you're up and running, Jim."

"I will, absolutely. We can work it through Pat again."

"Of course," Madeline said.

"That's a big move," Louis said, ever practical.

"Tell me about it," Jim said. "But when else am I going to do it? I've been working since I was twelve. Doing any and every kind of job you could imagine. And this is the only work I can truly say I love. I've loved every minute working on your house. You know how you get that feeling of being carried away when you really concentrate on something? This work does that for me. It's honest and fulfilling, and it sparked a passion I've been missing for a long time. Our kids are out of the house, so it's now or never. Is it crazy to start a business at fifty-three?"

"It's never too late to take a great opportunity. We're in somewhat the same boat ourselves."

Madeline added, "If you need help with finances, I know a guy." She leaned into Louis and patted his arm.

"The same for anything legal." Louis hugged Madeline closer to him.

Jim hadn't felt this good about a decision in a long time.

Reflection and Activity

Janelle, Louis, and Jim are all given incredible opportunities in this part of the story. Padme asks Janelle to help her put together and co-captain a soccer team, tasks at which Janelle excels. This may be just what she needs to follow Professor

Muñoz's advice to exercise more of her talents. Louis discusses with Madeline the opportunity Qasim has provided them both to give back to the community by helping establish and run a foundation for at-risk kids who love math and science and want to get into business. Jim explains his plans to start up Bulldog Fine Home Remodeling to Louis and Madeline, and their support helps him strengthen his will to step through that door.

Have you taken advantage of all the opportunities that have been available to you? Reflect on your life. Think about what doors have been open to you, what opportunities. Jot them down in two groups: the opportunities you took, and those you passed on.

Choose two or three of the more important opportunities you took, and explore them more deeply—those times you were mindful and took a risk. Then ask yourself these questions: What was the result of this opportunity? Did it work out the way you thought it would? If not, was it worse or better? By taking this opportunity, did you learn something about yourself? Did you realize you had a gift or talent or passion you weren't aware of? What emotions did you feel as you followed this opportunity? What was the impact of this opportunity on yourself and others? What else did you learn about yourself, emotionally, spiritually, intellectually?

Next, let's explore two or three doors you did *not* walk through. What held you back? Fear, hesitation, overthinking? Did you feel you weren't good enough to take that opportunity, that you didn't have the knowledge or skills you thought you needed? That it wasn't the right time or place?

Now fast-forward to the present day. Of the opportunities you chose not to take, are there some about which you can say, in all honesty and self-reflection, that you are glad you did not pursue them? We're not going to worry about those.

Let's turn to the opportunities you regret not taking. Given what you know today, how would you coach your younger self to reconsider the decision to pass by? Since we are nearing the end of the helm, what spokes would be helpful in making a better decision? Self-awareness, almost always. If you know you are risk averse, for example, but you also know you are being offered a great opportunity that involves some risk (a great job offer in another country, perhaps, or the opportunity to write a book!), how would you encourage yourself to take that risk? How could you be more mindful and responsive in a proactive way? You can actually use the helm to evaluate opportunities like these. Does the opportunity align with your greater purpose, your values, your passions, your talents? Do you know someone in your inner circle who can help you along on that journey, that decision? Will the opportunity raise you and others up? What's the worst-case scenario? Is that so bad?

The point of all this is to encourage you to be more receptive to the different paths that may open up for you in the future. How will you respond to them?

I often use a model called TOPs to demonstrate how opportunity intersects with two other important spokes of the helm, talent and passion. TOPs is an acronym for Talent, Opportunity, and Passions. When you leverage your talents and passions to create or respond to opportunities, you find yourself in the sweet spot: the intersection of all three. When you bring these elements together, you maximize your impact, which we'll discuss more in the next chapter.

To determine the intersection of talent, opportunity, and passion in your life, answer these questions regarding your conscious use of time:

1. In an average week, what percentage of time do you spend doing the things you love?

2. In an average week, what percentage of time do you spend doing the things you *must* do, things that you don't have a passion for—your duties and obligations?

3. In an average week, what percentage of time do you spend intentionally trying to learn, develop, and grow?

The first question represents the sweet spot (the intersection of talent, opportunity, and passion). The second question represents the intersection of talent and opportunity, and the third, the intersection of opportunity

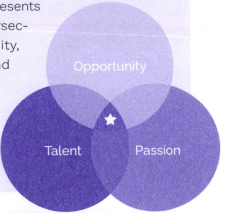

and passion. What's left? We come full circle to the intersection of passion and talent.

In fact, if you think about it, opportunity ties all the spokes of the helm together. Without stepping through the door of opportunity, you won't be able to pursue your purpose, become self-aware, determine your values, form a strong inner circle, follow your passion, exercise your talents, and create an impact. On the other hand, when you follow your passion, exercise your talents, pursue your life's purpose, and so on, you create opportunities for further growth. It's self-reinforcing.

It takes courage to venture into the unknown, to chart a course, to walk through the door, but it's well worth the effort. That's where you find Leading from the Helm's hidden treasure—a life of purpose and meaning.

Go to www.grabthehelm.com to enter your reflections and access more information.

CHAPTER 8

THE EIGHTH SPOKE OF THE HELM

IMPACT

*Never underestimate the valuable and important
difference you make in every life you touch.
For the impact you make today has a powerful
rippling effect on every tomorrow.*

—Leon Brown

We all encounter doors of opportunity, large and small, and when we are courageous enough to step through them, we can make an impact. Our impact is the result of everything we do. It is the difference we make in the world, the opportunities we open for others. The light we bring, the impressions we leave, the shadow that remains when we leave a room—these are our impacts.

It's easy to see how you impact yourself and others in the short term: the smile of gratitude on a neighbor's face when you bring them a homemade meal; the satisfaction of the A you receive after studying hard for an economics exam; the pleasure you get from the scent of the blossoming flowers you planted in the garden.

But there exists a greater impact, one you don't often get to see: the legacy you leave behind.

Legacy is your lasting impact, what you have sown and left behind for others to reap. But we don't always know what that legacy will be. We may want to think of ourselves as visionaries who can plan the ripples, the waves, we leave behind, but sometimes we can't foresee the magnitude of our impact—or what acts, large or small, have the greatest effect. That meal you made for your neighbor may turn out to be a favorite of their child's. They grow closer when they learn the recipe themselves, and it becomes one of their favorite family meals, giving pleasure for years to come. The economics class you aced may allow you to help a niece or nephew avoid an anxiety attack when they take the same class years later. The landscaping you worked so hard to craft in your yard might give the next homeowner great pleasure as they drink their coffee on the patio, the trees now ten feet higher than when you planted them.

We plant seeds now that we may never see grow to maturity and bear fruit. For this reason, we ought to make sure that these seeds have a positive result, since we don't know who will harvest them.

To make sure we plant seeds that bear nourishing fruit, we need good ground, a solid foundation—values, purpose, and passion, for example. But in addition, we must act with intention. We must be mindful of our passions and direct them in the right way, according to our values and purpose, by means of our natural talents and those we have developed. At the same time, we must be ready to take advantage of the opportunities we find in the moment that have immediate impacts as well as those of a deeper, more sustainable kind.

Think of your impact as the ripple in a pond or the butterfly effect—how something small we do right now can greatly affect someone or something else in a different place or time. What do you want to contribute to others? To the world? How do you handle this immense responsibility? Only by being mindful of your actions and exercising your talents and passions to influence others in a positive way; in short, by serving others. It may sound counterintuitive, but often you have the biggest impact not by forcing yourself to make one but simply by striving to serve.

JANELLE

It was the last Friday in October, and midterms had just wrapped up. No one Padme asked to be on the soccer team had dared turn her down, so they had put together a good group of men and women for afternoon practices leading up to today's game. Janelle had taken the lead on the workouts and practices; Padme had been the enforcer, making sure everyone showed up on time and ready to work; and Dionne had done the admin work, keeping track of the roster and filing the paperwork.

Janelle was pleased with the results so far, given that they hadn't had that much time to practice. They had some decent athletes for a music school, and everyone was so happy to be out of the practice rooms in the crisp fall air that they didn't complain about the drills and scrimmages Janelle put them through. Even Padme seemed to be enjoying herself. As co-captain, she wasn't shy about stepping in where she could help out. They worked pretty well together. What Janelle had taken in Padme for arrogance was really just a drive for excellence—something Janelle could well understand.

Today was their first game in the tournament, against the Divinity School. Janelle watched Div's pregame warm-ups while Padme took their own team through drills. The Divinity School seemed to know what they were doing. It would be a good test. She got those familiar pregame butterflies in her stomach, the same ones she got now before music performances.

"All right, everyone, bring it in. We'll go with the lineup we practiced yesterday, with Padme at center forward, and I'll take center midfield." In high school, Janelle had been center forward, also known as the striker—the best scorer on the team. In college she had stepped back to center midfield, where she could control the game more effectively and drop back to help on defense. "Jerry, you wanted left wing, yeah? So that puts you at right wing, Frieda. That okay?" Frieda nodded, taking a deep breath. Janelle was surprised by how seriously they were taking this. She hoped she had prepped them well—she didn't want to let them down. "In a game like this, defense is key." She nodded to her fullbacks—a woman and a man, a bass player and the kettle drummer, both a head taller than Janelle. They nodded their readiness. "And everyone else, don't try to do anything too fancy. When in doubt, kick it out and make them do a throw-in.

"Okay, I'll tell you what one of my coaches used to tell us before every game. Let's go out there and have fun. But it's a heckuva lot more fun to win!"

"Okay, hands in," Padme called out. "Beethoven on three." Janelle thought of how much her old teammates would've laughed at the chant, but she put her hand in with the others. "One-two-three-BEETHOVEN." They all raised their hands and cheered.

Dionne snuck in behind Janelle. She was dressed in gear and had taken part in the drills, but by her own request wasn't likely to play. "Killer cheer, Coach," she said, winking. "I haven't seen our class this excited since Professor Muñoz canceled class the week of her niece's wedding."

"Thanks, D. Here we go." The team jogged onto the field for the kickoff. The Divinity School had won the coin toss, so they got the ball to open the game. Janelle set everybody up in their defensive positions, and with the Divinity School's tap forward, the game was on.

The first half was rough, with both sides giving up and getting chances to score but no one succeeding. Janelle ran the offense from center midfield, but she was a little winded, not being in top shape, and too many of her passes were off the mark. Each of the front-line players managed shots on goal, but they all missed, with Padme coming closest, one shot banging off the side post and another off the crossbar.

At the half, the score was 0-0.

"Get some water and oranges," Janelle called at the break, a little breathless but exhilarated. What a great break from school.

Dionne walked around with a plastic bag of sliced oranges for anyone who wanted them.

"We're winning the field, but we've got to get it in the net," Janelle said to the team after she squirted water on her face. "Don't be so fine with the shots. Just bang them in there."

The front line nodded.

They settled down in the second half, playing more smoothly, and got their first score about ten minutes in on a throw-in from Janelle to Jerry, who crossed to Padme, who tapped to Frieda, who practically walked it into the goal.

"Nice job," Janelle said in the celebration huddle. "Keep the pressure on."

None of them were used to playing a full game, however, and it was starting to show. There was a great deal of standing around, heavy breathing, and tugging on their shorts, sure signs of fatigue. The best player on the Divinity squad stole the ball on a sloppy defensive exchange and scored on a breakaway. The score was 1-1, with about five minutes left to play.

Janelle huddled them briefly at the kickoff. "They're as tired as we are. We just need one." Then she pulled Padme and Frieda aside and said, "I've been saving this one—I can beat them down the right side. Padme, tap it to Frieda. Frieda, get it to me down the sideline. Then, Padme, be ready for the cross to the middle."

But Padme tapped it a little too far out in front of Frieda on the kickoff, and the defender was able to poke it away. Padme dashed after the ball and managed to control it, dribble around the defense, and punch it down the sideline to Janelle, who just did keep the ball in bounds. She deked the midfielder, then dribbled toward the right corner, anticipating at least two defenders. She knew Padme was caught up in the kickoff, so she was thinking she'd have to take the shot herself, difficult from that angle. In her peripheral vision, though, she saw Padme streaking down the center of the field. The defender went to Janelle's right foot, which was only natural, but Janelle put the ball on her left and kicked it around the defender, dropping it to Padme's right. Padme drilled it into the net.

The usually cool-headed Padme ran around in circles, then sprinted at Janelle, jumped into her arms, and knocked her to the ground. "How'd you do that? That pass was—amazing."

"You made the shot. Now let me up. We have to run out the clock."

Which they did. Energized by the goal, they were able to kill the clock by playing keep-away from their dispirited opponent. When the whistle blew for the end of the match, they lined up to congratulate the Divinity School, who were still shaking their heads about the pass and score.

The music team gathered on the sidelines, tired and elated both. "That was a *blast*," someone yelled out.

"Woot!"

"It *is* more fun when you win."

"Yeah, good job, everyone. Way to come together," Janelle said.

"Way to bring us together," Padme said, raising her bottle. "She's quiet in class, but she's killer on the field." Then more quietly, to Janelle, she said, "Seriously, you put some of that in your music and they'll name the auditorium after *you*."

"Thanks," Janelle responded. Was that what Professor Muñoz was trying to tell her? She'd have to think about it. "And midlevel, my foot. You were captain of your team, weren't you?"

"No," she said. "Maybe. Co-captain. Like now."

Janelle shook her head as they tapped water bottles.

Dionne popped in next to them. "Uh, roomie, don't you owe me something?"

"Yeah, I'm sorry you didn't get to play. Maybe next time."

"What? No! That looks like way too much work. I meant a ride home? We're both visiting our families this weekend?"

"Shoot, yeah. I forgot. We have to get on the road." Janelle looked around for her gear. Dionne handed her a duffel. "Oh, thanks. Gotta run, everyone. Have a great weekend. Practice on Monday."

"You too," a bunch of people yelled as Dionne and Janelle walked briskly toward their apartment.

"Hey, isn't this yours?" Padme called out.

Janelle spun around, walking backward. Padme held up the green-and-white hoodie Janelle had worn to the game.

"Hang on to it," she yelled back. "I'll grab it some other time."

LOUIS

Louis and Madeline had spent the previous two days getting the house ready for their dual celebration: Louis's retirement and a "basement warming" after the renovation, which had turned out better than they had hoped. Jim and his crew had taken Louis and Madeline's vision and suggested a few ideas of their own, combining traditional touches in the wood- and stonework and contemporary additions like the hidden TV and floor warmers. In essence, they'd created a whole new floor to the house, with cabin-style guest rooms, a huge new bathroom, an entertainment pod for watching movies, and a small kitchen.

It had been a while since the whole family had been together, and this was perfect timing before the holidays. The couple's two sons and daughters-in-law, Greg and Marcie, and Maurice and Tiana, would be there along with all five of their grandkids—that is, if Janelle could get away.

That mystery was solved fifteen minutes later when Janelle came in the through the mudroom the family always used. She was a bit out of breath.

"Janelle! You did make it." Louis hugged his granddaughter.

"I wouldn't miss it, Papa. You're always there for me."

Then he pulled away and sized her up. "With grass stains and a soccer uniform? What kind of music school is this?"

"Just taking a break from the grind." Janelle smiled.

"Looks like it's doing you a lot of good," Louis said.

"What are we, chopped liver?" her mother, Marcie, interjected, opening her arms next to Greg, her father.

Janelle ran over to hug her mom and dad. "No, of course not. I'm a little sweaty, though." Next she greeted her aunt and uncle and her cousins, all younger than she, then announced, "Let me grab a shower and I'll be right back. Is that okay, Gran?"

"Of course, of course. In fact, we'd prefer it," Madeline said, laughing. "I left some towels in the main bathroom upstairs. Don't use the white ones," she called out after Janelle had grabbed her bag and fled up the stairs.

This gave Louis time to catch up. "You must be proud of Janelle," Louis said to Greg and Marcie. "She's come a long way since the start of the program. She wasn't so sure of herself at first. She looks much happier than she sounded for a while."

"Yeah, thanks, Dad. You had a lot to do with that. We're just her dumb old parents, you know."

"The same way you thought about your mother and me, I'm sure."

"Maybe a little," he said, measuring it out with his thumb and forefinger. "Seriously, though, she's always looked up to you and you've had a big influence on the fine young woman she's growing into. If I don't say it enough, *thank you*. You and Mom are the best."

"What's that?" Louis said, holding his hand up to his ear. "I didn't quite hear you."

"You heard me fine," Greg said, punching Louis's arm and folding him into a hug.

"What did I miss?" Janelle said when she returned from her shower. She wore a nice pair of jeans, a cream white blouse, and a long flowy sweater tied at her waist.

"Don't you look nice," Madeline said.

Janelle did a mock curtsy and said, "Thanks, Gran."

Greg raised his glass and said, "A toast." When everyone settled down and faced him with their own glasses raised, he continued. "This day is about you, Dad. Thanks for giving us a great home and family and showing us how to make career and family work together. Congratulations on your retirement. It's well deserved. We love you."

"Hear, hear," was sprinkled in the background while everyone sipped at their glasses. Then the mandatory, "Speech, speech!"

Louis smiled. "That means so much to me, son. Thank you. And thank you all. There's no one I would rather share this with than those closest to me. I know some of you are concerned about how I'm going to occupy my time outside the glass office, but don't be. I've found the perfect hobby."

"Sudoku doesn't count," Greg hollered.

"No, it doesn't." Louis smiled. "I met a young man at work who's going to keep me quite busy running a foundation with him, and I'm going to do some speaking and mentoring at Harvey. He's here somewhere, I just heard someone let him in. Qasim? Where are you?"

Qasim stepped forward in jeans, a sci-fi T-shirt, and Chuck Taylor sneakers. With him was a man of about the same age, in a blue Oxford and dress jeans. "Everyone, this is Qasim and Jorge, Qasim's partner. Qasim, Jorge, this is everyone. I'll introduce you around when things settle down. Qasim, take a bow. This is one incredible young man, the one keeping me out of my easy chair. I wish I had a quarter of his energy. And Jorge's no slouch, either. He's wrapping up his PhD in interdisciplinary studies and is headed to Europe as a Fulbright scholar."

"That's great, guys," said Maurice. "You're keeping a better class of company these days, Dad."

"What kind of foundation?" Tiana asked.

"We're still working out the details, but it'll be to provide scholarships, fellowships, internships, and so on to young kids with a passion for economics and business who might otherwise not be able to afford to study those in high school and college. Your mother's going to be on the board."

"Wow, Dad, that's great," Greg said. "That'll have an impact."

"That's the idea, anyway."

Madeline hugged Louis with the arm that wasn't holding her glass. "We are all so proud of you."

The doorbell rang.

"I thought this was everyone," Janelle said, looking around the room. "Did we pick up more family while I was gone?"

"In a way," Louis said. "We got to know the guy who redid

the basement pretty well, so we invited him and his family for the grand opening. I hope nobody minds."

"Of course not, Dad. This is your day," Maurice said. Everyone else agreed.

"Can you do the honors?" he said to Janelle.

"Sure," she said, and trotted to the front door.

JIM

Jim, Shauna, and Dionne stood at the front door of the house where Jim had spent the last few weeks eating dust in the basement.

"Wow, Dad, you're moving up in the world," Dionne joked. She held the hostess gift, a basket of Thai spices.

"I just worked on the house, I didn't buy it." But he was proud that he had been able to "improve" such a historic home.

"I could get used to this," Shauna said, rubbing her hand on the heavy oaken door as it opened. She snatched her hand away just in time.

At the door stood a young woman Jim recognized but couldn't quite place. "Dionne, isn't that—"

"You've got to be kidding me!" the young woman at the door said, looking them over.

It was Janelle, Dionne's roommate, Jim remembered. He had just seen her when she had dropped Dionne off at the house not two hours before. Jim almost didn't recognize her out of context.

"What are you doing here?" Dionne said to her roommate.

"This is my grandparents' house. What are *you* doing here?" Janelle said.

"You mean my father remodeled your grandparents' basement? That's crazy. Dad, you never told me."

"I didn't know." Jim shrugged. He had been so focused on doing the job that he hadn't put two and two together.

"Please, please, c'mon in." Janelle shut the door behind them after they had moved into the foyer. "Nice to see you again, Mr. and Mrs. Riley," Janelle said awkwardly, perhaps remembering their last conversation.

"Don't worry, Janelle." Jim patted her on the shoulder to put her at ease, then gave her a hug. "I'm a changed man. Didn't Dionne tell you?"

"Yeah, I guess she did."

Jim stepped aside, and Dionne and Shauna each gave Janelle a hug in turn. Just then, Jim saw Louis striding into the foyer.

"Has the party moved in here?" Louis said. "Come in, come in. Let's get these jackets and things. Janelle, can you give me a hand?" He frowned at Janelle.

"Oh, no, don't blame her," Jim said. "She's in shock is all. We all are. These two know each other." Jim opened his hands and indicated his daughter and Janelle. Then he took his wife's jacket and laid it over Louis's outstretched arm. Dionne handed Janelle the gift basket.

"Papa, this is Dionne. My roommate. She's the one I've been telling you about."

"You mean the crazy one who hugs everyone," Madeline said, sweeping in from the other room. She gathered Dionne in her arms. "I love hugs. You're such a good friend to our granddaughter."

"And she to me," Dionne said.

Jim couldn't help but be proud.

"I know you," Madeline said, hugging Jim. "I can do that because you're not all grungy. And this must be your wife?"

"Yes, Shauna."

Madeline gave her a hug too.

"These are Madeline and Louis," Jim said. "My clients."

"Oh, friends, friends now, of course," Madeline said.

Jim was touched.

Louis said, "Jim has done a marvelous job on the house. We're recommending him to all our friends. He'll have plenty of work as soon as he's up and running. Come in and let me grab everyone some beverages."

Jim and his family followed Louis into the family room, where Louis made the introductions. Shauna moved in to chat with a woman about her age, Janelle's aunt, Jim guessed, and Dionne and Janelle were off in the corner catching up on the two hours they had been apart. Louis poured Jim an iced tea, which he gladly accepted. Since he was doing physical work again, he was always thirsty.

"I have to thank you again, Louis," Jim said. "Not just for welcoming me into your home to renovate your basement, but for the encouragement and referrals—not to mention Madeline's review of the paperwork. I filed yesterday. Bulldog Fine Home Remodeling is officially in business."

"I'm so glad," Louis said. "From this corner it looks like you're doing it the right way."

"It wasn't until working on your house that I saw how much a passion of mine could affect others' lives. Including mine." Jim wondered whether he should say what else was on his mind, then found the courage and decided to go ahead. "You know, you and Madeline are a big inspiration to me— you've had more of an influence than I think I can really express. Just the way you handle yourselves, the way you are clearly crazy about each other but have your own things going on." He was close to choking up. "It's just that—that's it.

You're an inspiration." Jim was embarrassed. He usually wasn't this sentimental.

Louis grabbed him by the arm and said, "Thank you. Truly. Now let's go see what the family thinks of your work. They're the ones who count." He turned to the group, cupped his hands around his mouth, and announced, "Time for the unveiling."

Jim held back to let the family go down the stairs. One thing the crew had done was widen the stairway and create more headroom.

"Hey, I don't bang my head anymore." That sounded like Greg.

"Nor do I." That must have been Louis.

Jim was a little nervous, actually. Would the rest of the family like what they had done as much as Louis and Madeline had?

Once Jim made it down the stairs, he saw the group gathered loosely in the area in front of the fireplace. Above the fireplace, Jim knew, was the hidden TV that doubled as a gaming and presentation screen. The fireplace itself was covered with cardboard, and the new kitchen and bedrooms were concealed behind drop cloths hung from the ceiling.

"Everybody make it down?" Louis called out. "Okay, good. Everyone gather around." Since Louis was facing the fireplace, everyone else had gathered in a half circle facing that way as well. "Jim, where's Jim? Come up here, front and center." Louis waved Jim over with the tablet he was holding.

The group parted, and Jim worked his way up front, taking his place next to Louis.

"We owe everything you are about to see to this man and his crew. At work, I am—well, *was*—known for my brisk meetings. So without further ado…"

Louis pressed the tablet. The wooden panels above the fireplace slid sideways in opposite directions. The crowd went "Ahhhh." On the screen it read: "Welcome to the new Williams Basement. Thank you, Jim and Crew." It showed the crew as cartoon characters and listed all their names.

Then animated figures of Louis and Madeline cut a ribbon with a huge pair of scissors, and Louis announced, "The Williams family basement is officially open for *fun!*"

He nodded to the younger grandkids, with whom he had clearly made arrangements. They pulled down the drop cloths to reveal the lodge-style kitchen and bedrooms. Louis himself pulled away the cardboard from the fireplace. The adults let out another round of "Ahhhs."

"Credit where credit is due—I did not make that animation, Qasim did." He opened his hand to indicate Qasim, who bowed dramatically. Jorge tapped him on the arm. "Ham!"

Louis caught the grandchildren's eyes. They gathered up the drop cloths and cardboard and put them in what Jim knew to be the storage room.

Meanwhile, everyone else was buzzing with appreciation, walking around, admiring the work that had been done. Dionne and Shauna were standing together, looking around in amazement. Jim walked up behind them and put his hand on their shoulders. "Wow, Dad," Dionne said. "You did all this?"

"Sure," Jim said. "But not alone. I had the crew. And don't sound so surprised."

"He fixed the hole in the wall from that time I threw a baseball," Greg said. "But there it is imprinted in the tile on the fireplace."

"And look what else," Janelle said. "All our names are carved in the brick." Janelle ran her fingers over each name.

"My signature surprise," Jim announced.

"Oh, Dad, that was so bad!" Dionne exaggerated a face palm.

"You kept the original wood from the time we tried to build that tree house," Greg said. "Wow, I forgot about that."

Louis turned to Jim. "Thank you for what you did for our family, Jim. You helped preserve our memories and those of the people I care most about. They feel a part of this house even when they're off being superstars." Louis smiled at Janelle. "What a nice mark to leave. Here's hoping it stays in the family for generations to come."

For once Jim the salesman didn't know what to say. He simply mouthed, "No—thank you."

"Enough of this sentimentality," Louis announced. "The food isn't going to eat itself. Dig in." He indicated the trays of food laid out on the kitchen counter.

And Jim did just that, filling his plate with some of the snack foods—mini tacos, Thai spring rolls, stuffed mushrooms, and a scoop of fruit salad. Before he began eating, however, he took a moment for gratitude. He was honored to have made a difference, grateful that working on Louis and Madeline's house had helped him reenergize his life. He chuckled to himself at his next thought. His legacy had been helping Louis and Madeline create their own.

Reflection and Activity

By the choices they make and the opportunities they pursue, Janelle, Louis, and Jim all have profound impacts on their own growth and the growth of others. When Janelle agrees to co-captain the music program's soccer team, she breaks open a logjam of self-doubt while giving her colleagues a break from their demanding program as well as the opportunity to share team spirit. In gathering friends and family to celebrate his retirement, the basement renovation, and the foundation, Louis acknowledges the importance of impact and legacy. His friends and family honor him in return for what he has given them. Jim is touched by the gratitude shown by the whole Williams family for his work preserving their family heritage—not only the house but the memories as well.

Here's a thought experiment: What would your legacy be right now, this instant? What impact have you had on the world? If you're drawing a blank, that's okay. This can be a daunting question. Let's work our way through it.

First, ask yourself what decisions and actions of yours have had a positive impact. Write down all you can think of.

Next, write down examples of negative impacts you might have had. It's important to be honest— self-aware—and acknowledge both sides.

Now let's turn to legacy. What do you want your long-term legacy or legacies to be? What do you think they will be? Have you been fortunate enough to see some of your influence come to fruition in your lifetime? Perhaps you coach youth volleyball or volunteer at a food bank, or you have set up college funds for your children or grandchildren, nieces or nephews.

What about legacies you have received? Have you had the benefit of harvesting the fruit of seeds others have planted? Mentors? Benefactors? Grandparents or other relatives? Is there a person or event that has changed the course of your life? Acknowledge these with gratitude.

Though chance sometimes plays a role, legacy and impact are too important to be left to chance completely. We must think about them with intention. What am I contributing that can benefit others, whether that's something tangible like money or intangible like love, support, understanding? Yes, I can do something right now that provides myself or others satisfaction, but how will my actions have an effect two weeks, two months, or two years from now?

Given what you've become aware of about your passions, talents, and purpose, what opportunities do you have today to chart your course to achieve the influence you desire? Be mindful of the impacts your decisions and actions might have. Be intentional about your legacy. But keep in mind that impact often starts with service.

Holocaust survivor and author of *Man's Search for Meaning,* Viktor Frankl, puts it this way: "Everyone has his own specific vocation or mission in life; everyone must carry out a concrete assignment that demands fulfillment. Therein he cannot be replaced, nor can his life be repeated, thus, everyone's task is unique as his specific opportunity to implement it."

You offer something unique and personal to this world. Sometimes you have a clear vision of what that positive impact can be, and you plan toward it; other times you simply speak from the heart: *I want to help, but I don't yet know how or where.* This kind of mindfulness and intention opens you to many opportunities to make a real contribution.

You shouldn't focus solely on the results, though. Making a difference is as much a state of mind as it is a specific outcome. When you lead a life of purpose driven by your values, passions, and talents, you can't help but affect your life and the lives of others in small and large ways. You open opportunities for yourself and others to grow. This is service. When you concentrate on serving others—your family, your crew, the world at large—the results will follow, and you will light the way for others to follow, too.

Go to www.grabthehelm.com to enter your reflections and access more information.

CHAPTER 9

GRAB THE HELM
PURPOSE REFINED

Realize deeply that the present moment is all you ever have. Make the Now the primary focus of your life.

—Eckhart Tolle

Some of us have always known our purpose. It's on our minds all the time. It's what drives us, what gets us up in the morning. Some of us have found our purpose along the way, by means of a particular person or event, an epiphany, an awakening. And some of us may have come to this book with little idea about our purpose or what it even means to live a life of purpose. Don't worry. Wherever you fall on this spectrum, you're in the right place.

What is important to understand is that our purpose is not written in stone. As we turn the helm and experience all its spokes, we may very well change our purpose from time to time. The purpose of a twenty-five-year-old graduate student is different from that of a fifty-three-year-old middle manager, which is different from that of a seventy-year-old retiree.

In this way, a life of purpose is a daily journey, a daily awakening, a daily questioning about how we want to live right now, today, in this moment. Life will throw us curves (also known as opportunities) that we may not think we are ready for. These curves may knock us off balance, force us to question our purpose, to reconsider our lives. Are we doing it wrong? Or maybe what we were absolutely convinced was The Purpose simply doesn't suit the circumstances of our lives any longer. That's okay. That's part of the journey. What that means is that it's time to refine our purpose. Even if we don't know the next step exactly, if we have the courage to reset our course by walking through a new door of opportunity, and by coming to a new awareness of self, our new purpose will be revealed.

Here's my advice to you. Guided by your values, passions, and talents, be ready to pivot when the winds change, and be ready to step into those new opportunities you suddenly see in front of you—or behind you or to the side or across the lake—those opportunities that just might send you in an entirely different direction to live an entirely new purpose.

JANELLE

Twenty-Two Years Later

Janelle had conducted the city orchestra for its normal Tuesday night rehearsal. Afterward the group had surprised her with cake and candles and of course their rendition of "Happy Birthday," with a few orchestral flourishes. It was her forty-seventh birthday. She was touched they had remembered.

"How old are you, Maestra?" a clarinet player teased. "Or don't you want to say?"

"Knock it off with the *Maestra*. I'm forty-seven and proud of it. Never apologize for your mileage," she said louder, for the rest of the group. "Time is a gift." Janelle blew out the candles on the sheet cake, accepted a knife, and sliced the cake into pieces for serving.

After graduating with her MFA, Janelle had moved to New York City with Dionne, where they continued as roommates for several years until they each found partners. They were still best friends and kept in touch in all the usual ways. Dionne toured as a concert pianist and texted Janelle at three in the morning with a cheery, "I have no idea what time it is there. Can you talk?" Janelle was usually able to put her off for a couple of hours.

Though she never did play with the New York Philharmonic, Janelle never had to work as anything other than a musician. She was able to live comfortably, as much as one could in New York, and travel across the globe playing the violin. When she was home, she gave lessons.

The highlight of her career had been performing at Carnegie Hall, and with a jazz orchestra no less. She had received a desperate call from Professor Muñoz one night (Janelle had never learned to call her by her first name). Professor Muñoz was on yet another retirement tour, as she called her performances, and one of her violinists had come down with the flu and couldn't get out of bed. Could Janelle please, please, do a friend a solid and fill in?

Would she? Janelle had said. When and where? Carnegie Hall? Talk about burying the lede!

After one encore—Professor Muñoz always had several—the professor told the story of an old student of hers who froze during improv one day and was this close to quitting (the professor did like to exaggerate) until she let that student know how music comes from the soul, from the whole person, and above all, how music is supposed to be fun—and look where she is now. Aren't we having fun? She had Janelle stand up and take a bow to the clapping crowd, then launched into one of her classics. Janelle could barely see the sheet music with the tears in her eyes.

After a few years in New York, Janelle met her husband, Jeremy. Two kids later, they decided to trade in the bustling city life for a quieter and easier home in which to raise their family. What better place than Janelle's hometown? And what better home than her grandparents', which she had inherited when they passed away in their eighties? That was how Janelle found herself back in the Midwest, this time with a family, a career, and a purpose—though it was a slightly different purpose than when she had set out on her musical journey more than twenty years before.

Janelle still missed her grandparents as if they had passed yesterday. In their honor, she filled their old home with laughter and music. She hadn't forced her kids to play, but they came by it naturally, her daughter, Madeline, the singer and pianist (like Dionne), her son, Jamal, all things strings—classical violin, cello, fiddle, bass, guitar, mandolin, banjo, pedal steel guitar. Depending on the day, he was a one-man orchestra or medicine show.

Janelle also honored her grandparents by sitting on the board of the foundation they had founded with Qasim, though she left the day-to-day running to Qasim and Jorge's two sons, whom they had adopted as foster children. In the last twenty years, the foundation had given out hundreds of scholarships and fellowships and funded internships at companies all over the country.

Dionne's father, Jim, who had remodeled Janelle's grandparents' basement so many years before, was in his seventies and still owned Bulldog Fine Home Remodeling. He had several younger partners and only did the most creative jobs. Since the house was even older now, Janelle hired Jim's company from time to time. Jim always did that work himself.

Janelle had always dreamed of living in New York City and playing in the orchestra until she was eighty, but life had brought her much broader horizons filled with many more opportunities. If Professor Muñoz and her improv class had taught her anything, it was to be open to the moment. Once she had learned to be more open—a lesson she had to teach herself time and again—she had discovered a host of other talents, as a mother, a teacher, a conductor, a leader. When her vision expanded, her talents expanded with it. But at the center of it all was her love for music. The older she grew, the more important it was for her to share that gift.

Janelle beamed, looking around the room at the thirty musicians who had just performed "Happy Birthday." She had conducted this orchestra for the last seven years and cared about each member dearly. A few had come and gone, but many had been with her the whole time.

As she sat down to enjoy her red velvet cake, Rahim, one of the newer members, came up to her. Rahim had joined the company only a few months before. A prodigy, he was sixteen and an excellent flautist. He was quiet, though, so Janelle didn't know much about him.

"Excuse me, uh, Ms. Williams?" he said.

"Hi, Rahim," Janelle answered, setting down her plastic fork onto the paper plate. Janelle still used her family name professionally. "How are you?"

"Er—fine," Rahim said.

Janelle smiled, allowing him his own time to settle in and speak.

"Everyone here is very talented," he said finally.

"And so are you."

"I know," he said, to Janelle's surprise. She had expected a more modest response. "Everyone has been telling me that my whole life. It's like I was born to do this or something."

"And you don't agree?"

"I'm just not sure music is what I want to do. But how can I say that? I'm only sixteen. What do I know, really?"

"Being sixteen doesn't have anything to do with it," Janelle responded. "Nor does being seventy or twenty-five or forty-seven. It's never too early or too late to decide what you like and don't like doing—what your purpose is."

"It's just, my whole family are musicians. They're not the best teachers, though, so my mom wanted me to study under you because she knows how great you are."

Janelle wondered who his mother was but held back from asking. Rahim seemed to feel safe enough to confide in her. She didn't want to scare him away.

"I mean, it makes me happy," he continued, "for now, but why put so much time into something I might not do for the rest of my life?"

"Because it makes you happy?" Janelle responded. Rahim didn't seem satisfied with that answer, so she went on. "I used to overplan my life," Janelle said. "Everything I did was in service of just one goal. But I eventually realized I didn't want my life to be one conquest after another. Because if you view life like that, you'll never really find what you're looking for. There's always another conquest around the corner."

Rahim stared at the floor.

"Does music give you joy?"

"I guess," Rahim said. "I love coming here every Tuesday. I like seeing all my friends. I like playing the music. It's a good release."

"So then keep doing it."

This seemed to frustrate Rahim. "That's what I've been trying to tell you. I feel like doing this is distracting me from what I'm supposed to be doing with my life."

"And what are you supposed to be doing with your life?"

Rahim became embarrassed. "I don't know. I'd kinda like to do something with money, you know, finance."

"My grandfather loved finance," Janelle said wistfully. "And I have an idea. But hold on. Let me say this first. We have two seasons in this city, Rahim. Do you know what they are?"

Rahim shook his head.

"Winter and construction season."

Rahim smiled at the joke.

There was something familiar about that smile, but Janelle couldn't place it. "Think of it this way. Your life mission, your purpose, whatever you want to call it—it's like a highway always under construction. It's always in draft form. You really limit yourself if you become too narrowly focused. You won't discover everything today. I can't tell you what your life is going to look like, Rahim, but the most important piece of advice I can give you is to live in the present. Live in the now. Enjoy your Tuesday nights playing the flute. Don't tell yourself you have to play the flute every Tuesday night for the rest of your life. Focus on this Tuesday, and maybe the next one. You are the author of your own life."

"I'm sure you're right, though I don't like construction, or winter for that matter."

Janelle laughed. "Let me put it another way. You're sixteen. And you've charted this whole course for your life. But winds change, and being able to notice these changes and adjust your sails, take a different tack, is critical. Otherwise you shut yourself off to great opportunities."

Janelle could tell she was losing the poor kid in her metaphors.

"Look, I thought I *knew* exactly where I would end up. But I embraced the changes that came my way, and I am so grateful for the life I've had so far, a life my twenty-year-old self never really pictured."

"I get it. I just already feel this pressure to have everything figured out."

"I completely understand. Many of us feel that way at some point. But every day is an evolution. We are all constantly developing and growing. You're already on the right track because you're asking the right questions. But make sure you never lose the now, Rahim. You only have it once. One of my favorite teachers reminded me of that all the time. Just keep doing what you love, and your purpose will reveal itself."

A car honked outside. "I think that's my mom," Rahim said, gathering his sweatshirt, bag, and flute case.

"Wait," Janelle said. "My idea." She found a pen and notepad in her bag, wrote out a name and telephone number. "I'm on a board of a foundation that raises money for at-risk kids interested in economics and business." She ripped off the sheet of paper and held it out to Rahim.

He pulled his hand away.

"No, no, I'm not saying I think you're at risk. Sorry. I wasn't clear. How'd you like an internship at the foundation? For high schoolers. In finance. Call that number for an interview, but give me a few days to arrange it, okay?"

"There's an opening?"

"I'm pretty sure there is. I just created the position. But I've been thinking about it for a while."

Rahim looked up at Janelle with surprise, then genuine gratitude. "I don't know what to say."

"Thank you will do just fine. And coming to rehearsal. Now scoot. Don't keep your mother waiting."

"Okay, thank you. And thanks for listening. And for the advice. And the interview, of course." Rahim pulled on the sweatshirt and went out the door with a bounce in his step. He looked back over his shoulder. "Happy birthday."

With a shock, Janelle recognized the green-and-white hoodie—the one she had never remembered to retrieve all those years before, the one she had accidentally lent to a talented and severe violinist who had terrified Janelle until she had gotten to know her on the soccer field. Rahim and Padme looked so much alike now that she knew.

She'd have to give Padme a hard time for not saying hello. But not tonight. Tonight was perfect as it was, and doubly so now that she was reminded of that soccer game their first year, where Padme had tackled her to the ground after scoring the winning goal, a moment of pure joy for both of them. Janelle always said that that was the day that broke the logjam, that taught her to take things as they came, to get joy out of every moment, to play her music with the same abandon she played soccer. That was the day that led her to this moment, right here, pursuing her passions in a life of purpose she never could have imagined twenty-two years before.

Reflection and Activity

The helm is a constantly moving wheel. Each spoke is connected with the others, and only when they are used as one can they steer our course toward our purpose.

Now that you've read the story and completed the reflections and exercises in the book, what have you discovered? Did you have an aha moment inspired by a particular spoke of the helm or one of the characters or events in the story? Did one spoke in the helm speak to you more than the others? Are you confident in your passions but questioning your values? Do the spokes suggest areas of self-improvement, things you can work on? Your crew? Self-awareness? Opening yourself to the doors of opportunity? (Almost everyone can do better with that.)

As I mentioned in the opening to this chapter, the search for purpose involves *daily* discovery. To make this journey of discovery, we must cultivate awareness, mindfulness, curiosity, and courage. Without these traits, we wander off course or ground ourselves on the rocks of uncertainty.

Here are some concrete reminders to help you stay on course:

Know thyself: Understand your personality style, your energies, how you uniquely experience the world (*Self-Awareness*). Determine your core values, the cornerstones of your belief system (*Values*). Only when you are completely aware of yourself are you able to build trust and make connections with others.

Understand others: When you know yourself, you can begin to know others and build trust with them. You can see the beauty in others and acknowledge what they have to offer the world. Be open and willing to learn from them (however different they may be from you) and welcome them on your life journey while you support theirs (*Crew*).

Know what you love and love what you know: Be aware and accepting of your passions—this is your fuel and what brings you joy. Don't be afraid to follow your passions, and be open to the new ones that come along (*Passion*). Grow, grow, grow, and grow some more. Develop your natural gifts, and stretch yourself by expanding your skills and knowledge (*Talent*).

Chart a course: Look, be present, be mindful of every moment and opportunity. You have no idea when you will get the next chance to live by your talents, passions, and purpose. Look for doors that are opening, and, just as important, acknowledge doors that are closing. Be ready to adjust your sails (*Opportunity*).

Sow your seeds: Let the fruits of your labor grow naturally by doing the things you love. Be intentional about the legacy you want to leave, but also understand that serving others is the surest road to making a contribution (*Impact*).

When you follow the spokes of the helm, you will not be forced to struggle in search of your purpose; your purpose will find you, it will be revealed. Leading from the Helm is a model and process that benefits you at any age and in any circumstance. Conduct your journey to purpose by following the compass of your unapologetic passions, governed by your unique talents, steadfast values, and greater understanding of yourself, and with your crew by your side. The helm will always be there for you to grab on to if you've lost the way. You have much to offer this world, and I sincerely hope we all get to experience it. Go out and live your purpose-filled life.

CONCLUSION

CHARTING YOUR COURSE

The privilege of a lifetime is being who you are.
—Joseph Campbell

The summer after our death-defying voyage in the North Atlantic, I met up with Dave for another leg of the journey. With a year of sailing under my belt, I was excited to get back on *The North Star* to show what I could do. I imagined Marcella rolling her eyes at my decision, and I realized in all the craziness the previous year, I had never let her know we were okay.

The North Star was docked at Sodus Point on Lake Ontario, about thirty-five miles from Rochester, New York. We wasted no time getting underway, stopping only in Niagara Falls for a night to have a nice dinner and spend a day as tourists. The next morning we rose before the sun and started our journey south down the Welland Canal, which connects Lake Ontario and Lake Erie, allowing ships of all kinds and sizes to avoid the falls. The canal consists of eight locks. The first seven are closer to Lake Ontario in the north, and we went through those fairly quickly. It took us the rest of the day to make our way down the rest of the canal until we came to the last lock, with Lake Erie nearly in sight.

It was 4:00 p.m. when we finally made it through the canal. Lake Erie looked like glass, calm and quiet. The weather was perfect, with enough wind to move us along, but no storms in sight—quite the contrast from our trip the year before.

Dave noticed how I was looking at the lake in awe. He chuckled before saying, "You want to sail it, don't you? Right now."

"What?" I snapped out of my trance.

"You want to pull an all-nighter." It was a statement more than a question.

The huge smile on my face was enough of an affirmation for Dave.

"All right, let's go," he said.

After a quick shower and a much-needed dinner, we got underway around six. Dave and I hung out on the deck for a few hours until he went below and slept the whole night. He was not as keen to stay up as I was.

So there I was, hand at the helm again, excited but

anxious for what the night would bring. But this time there was no rain or huge rollers, and the wind was easy, the sky clear and filled with stars. All the technology was working—the warning systems, the compasses, the electricity, autopilot. I laughed at the extreme contrast to our last experience. I went on to have the easiest, most beautiful twelve hours of night sailing in my life.

We sailed twenty-seven straight hours across Lake Erie until we arrived in Sandusky, Ohio. We rested a bit, and from there we went up to Detroit. Then, by way of the Detroit River, we sailed into Lake Saint Clair, sometimes called the sixth Great Lake, a smaller lake between Lake Erie and Lake Huron. This was where Dave and I parted ways.

Though Dave went on to finish his journey to Duluth, Minnesota, the following summer, this was the end of my part in Dave's Great Lakes adventure, but not the end of the impact that voyage had on my life. I am grateful to this day that Dave invited me to accompany him as first mate, both in honor of my brother Tom and because it became one of the indelible experiences of my life. This is what I mean when I talk about having the courage to open yourself to opportunity. What if I had said to Dave, "No, sorry, sounds like fun, but I've got too much going on"? I would have passed up one of the most transformative experiences of my life.

*

I'm sure I got my love for night sailing from my brother Tom. He loved to sail at night together. I could always get him to go out as long as we had even just a sliver of moon.

Before he passed, Tom had given me one of his many sailboats, a seventeen-footer without a weighted keel. I kept it out on a lake near Minneapolis for two summers so my niece, a competitive sailor, could use it. But in the end, it was a racing boat and not very stable. I asked my nieces, Tom's daughters, Hannah and Brita, if it was all right to sell it. With their approval, I traded it in for an easier-to-handle eighteen-foot wing-keeled daysailer, which we named *Lil' Tommy*.

When the weather is nice, and the Minnesota lakes aren't frozen, I sail *Lil' Tommy* on Buffalo Lake two or three times a week. I often invite family members to join me, usually my mom and sisters (and of course my dad when he was alive). We've sailed it during family reunions and birthdays—and any other time we were all itching to get out. I love that my family can enjoy the boat and get a taste of the sailing Tom and I loved so much. But I most enjoy going out at night to sail under the light of the moon with only my dog, Miss Mia Luna, as my companion. It reminds me of all the journeys I've been on, the crazy and the calm, and the gratitude I have for the times I shared with my brother before he passed away.

*

Tom's legacy exists in that little boat on Buffalo Lake but also in the construction company he left behind. Before he passed, Tom painstakingly interviewed dozens of people to take over Sicora Design & Build. After passing on many qualified candidates, he finally settled on a house inspector named Ron. It shocked me. Ron could not have been more different than Tom. Where Tom was loud, Ron liked to think things through and keep to himself a bit more. Where Tom needed to be everywhere all at once with his hands in everything, Ron thought delegating was a more efficient way to get things done. Where Tom intentionally kept the firm small because it would take too much out of him if it grew too large, Ron had a vision for expanding the business. Despite their differences, Tom trusted Ron.

Ron engaged me and the rest of Sicora Consulting to make sure my brother's good work continued after the transfer of ownership. We conducted workshops based on Leading from the Helm that helped the team build trust and engagement by understanding the firm's strategies, values, processes, and culture. As always, we emphasized how everyone has leadership within them so that employees and leaders could both leverage their innate strengths to increase personal performance and that of the firm. We held on to the good things and purged what was no longer needed. Sicora Design & Build came out stronger on the other side.

Now, more than ten years after my brother's passing, Sicora Design & Build has gone on to flourish and become an even larger part of the Twin Cities community. The firm has grown beyond what Tom ever thought possible and continues to make a daily impact in the lives of the people it serves.

I'm inspired by my brother's legacy, and it often makes me think about my own. I see now that this book is part of my legacy. By writing *Grab the Helm*, I hope to offer individuals a process for self-reflection, for figuring out who they are, what they care about, what they love, and who they want to serve. I want to inspire readers to be curious about how they engage with others and why, what they live for, and how they act on this knowledge.

These are questions I ask myself daily. Although the lives of Janelle, Louis, and Jim are fictional, they are based on real people and real experiences, including some of my own.

I strive to practice Leading from the Helm daily. Perhaps sharing my personal journey with the helm in my own life will give you some ideas of how to use it effectively in yours.

Purpose

My purpose has always been to guide individuals and organizations to become the best versions of themselves. Since I was seventeen, I have recognized that we all have aha moments in our lives—epiphanies or awakenings—when we realize all the things we are capable of; when we become motivated to maximize the impact we can have on the world. But when does this lightbulb turn on for us? Can we control the switch?

In my early twenties, I worked as a recreational therapist with teenagers and adults stuck in chemical dependency or caught up in massive victimization. It's hard enough for a happy, healthy person to find purpose and meaning, but how could I help these people in deep pain find a way for the lightbulb to come on?

That is where it started for me, and from that point on, I've dedicated myself to creating opportunities for anybody and everybody to transcend their limits, to gain awareness, and to find their passion and purpose. That is my passion and purpose: helping others come to that enlightenment, that aha moment, while also giving them the opportunity and tools to follow through. In this way, I hope to inspire everyone to create a life of purpose beyond anything their self-imposed limitations have allowed them to believe.

Self-Awareness

Remember the four color energies?

Red energy = Expressive thinking

Yellow energy = Expressive feeling

Blue energy = Reflective thinking

Green energy = Reflective feeling

Anyone who knows me knows that I love expressing ideas as they come into my head. In that way, I almost always lead with Red energy—expressive thinking. What's my second energy? In my corporate years, I was very conscientious and thoughtful, so I combined Red and Blue energies. Now that I am a facilitator of understanding and change with a passion to engage with individuals and organizations, I have transitioned to leading more often with Red/Yellow energies—pure extroversion. But remember, we all have all four colors within us, and the most important work I've done on my own self-awareness in the past ten years is what is called shadow work, our relationship with our least preferred color—in my case, Green, reflective feeling.

I know I lead with Red energy by default. I know I go deep Blue when I am collecting data and in a conscientious mindset with my clients. I know that I lead with Yellow energy when I am facilitating and speaking. But it is the profound experiences I had with my brother and father that inspire me to go deep within my Green energy. In this I am emulating my late father, Papa Tom, who almost always led with a profound Green energy. I admired my dad for being so open and vulnerable in sharing himself with others. Ever since my brother passed, I noticed how little I had been exercising this part of myself. Because I don't want to cut myself off from any part of the human experience, I've been working on exploring Green energy—learning to balance all four energies within me.

Values

I value relationships, consistency, and building trust. I wrote my doctoral dissertation on trust research, specifically on determining how, by understanding our own personality styles and developing social and emotional intelligence, we can adapt to the personality styles of others in order to help them feel comfortable, safe, and willing to be vulnerable with one another. This is how you build strong, trusting, lasting relationships, and for me, there is nothing more important than trusting relationships. Further, this research has helped me understand how to acknowledge, develop, and live in integrity with my own values.

Crew

As it was for my father, my immediate crew, my inner circle, is my family. I have my son and seven siblings and their children, my many nieces and nephews. Having them close is important to me, and when that is not physically possible (because I am the hugger in the family), I touch base with them as often as I can by all the means available in the twenty-first century, including Sunday afternoon Zoom calls.

My Leading from the Helm crew at Sicora Consulting is critical as well—Adam, Erin, Ian, Jason, Laura, Mary, and others, who help create this community of practice. They provide a diversity of perspective and give me that combination of feedback and support we all need to grow.

And now I'd like to extend an invitation to you, to everyone reading this book—the individuals looking for personal growth, the leaders striving to help their organizations become more efficient and effective, everyone who wants to become part of Leading from the Helm, this open source of inspiration and development. My crew extends to you.

Passion

In addition to sailing, travel, and playing sports, my love and passion are in building engagement *with* others and inspiring engagement *in* others—a critical quality for a facilitator, consultant, and speaker. By engagement, I mean relationship, connection, and intellectual and emotional commitment to what you are doing and who you are doing it with. At the core of engagement is a kind of joy, that sense of flow you get when you mindfully throw yourself into the task at hand, whether that task be an activity or a conversation. In organizations, engagement means enthusiasm and productivity; for individuals, it means joy, bliss, happiness.

For this reason, I get immense satisfaction and joy from helping others learn to be present and fulfilled in what they're doing, not just in the workplace, but also in life. To guide them, I developed a model called the 8 Factors of Engagement, which helps maximize engagement in work and in life:

> **Purpose:** What you are passionate about and how it aligns with what you do.
>
> **Agility:** How flexible you are in the face of change.
>
> **Recognition:** We all want to be recognized and acknowledged for our accomplishments, but it begins within. Acknowledge your own victories and accomplishments, and external recognition will follow.
>
> **Care:** Care about the people you work with and those you serve in and out of the workplace.

Trust: Build trusting relationships both in and outside of work.

Development: Take—and create—opportunities to grow your talents and skills.

Resources: Make sure you have the right information and the right people in your crew to attain your goal.

Accountability: Establish clear expectations and high standards for yourself and others. Then meet and exceed those expectations when you can.

When we implement this model with individuals, teams, and organizations, we've found an interesting result: *that simply introducing this model inspires engagement.* Once you start thinking about these themes, you are by definition engaged, and the more you think about them, the more engaged you become.

It's wonderful to see the lightbulb go on, and I am grateful that I can see my passion for engagement take root and grow in my work with others.

Talent

I was a fast runner as a younger man, I'm a good sailor (regardless of what Dave says), and I'm a creative chef, but the talent I am most proud of and the one I exercise most often is systems thinking. I've always been able to see how things fit together and to create models, such as Leading from the Helm, that show others how they do. (I've also worked on developing this talent by getting a master's and a doctorate.)

These gifts allow me to develop these models into tools that are helpful and engaging at the same time. In this book

I've referred mostly to models that work well for the personal development, such as the eight spokes of the individual helm, the Four Colors of Insights, and the 8 Factors of Engagement I just mentioned. Other models, of which I am also proud, are more useful in an organization setting, including the Purposeful Culture of Trust, the Transformational Leadership model, and the Team Effectiveness model.

It is in this gift for systems thinking that my passion and talents align, and I am grateful that I have found a purpose that gives me the opportunity to practice these skills every day.

Opportunity

Many great opportunities have opened to me and Sicora Consulting because of the invitations I've had to speak and share all we have to offer. Some of these doors I've worked to open for myself, while gracious referrals have opened many others.

This book might be one of my biggest opportunities. My hope for *Grab the Helm* is that it fulfills my purpose of guiding individuals and organizations to become the best versions of themselves by reaching a greater number of people. I want everyone who is willing and courageous enough to grab the helm to have the opportunity to do so.

Impact

In my work, I've seen incredible transformations of organizations' cultures that were toxic, distrustful, and actively disengaged. With the help of Sicora Consulting, these organizations turned around in nine to eighteen months. It is rewarding to check in with them and see how much healthier their culture has become and how much happier their employees are—which leads to greater productivity and return on investment.

As I mentioned in the introduction, in the course of our work with organizations, we discovered that the concepts of Leading from the Helm can transform the lives of individuals as well. With this book we are planting the first seeds of this new opportunity. I ask for your help in spreading these seeds widely so that as many as possible can reap the fruit and experience this transformational journey. That is the impact, the legacy, that I hope to leave behind.

Purpose Refined: The Journey Continues

As I stand at the helm every day, I reflect on all the spokes to remind myself what my purpose is and why I am doing it. My purpose is to provide individuals, teams, and organizations the opportunity to better understand themselves and each other—both individually and collectively—then align to establish a shared purpose that produces the greatest positive impacts to the communities they serve. I hope to help you uncover the aha moments, to help you see the doors of opportunity and step through them without fear or hesitation. I want you to have the ability to chart the course to your true potential. In short, I want you to experience a life far beyond what you may have previously imagined.

Though I have a strong sense of purpose, I am constantly learning, still figuring out the course of my journey. I didn't think that picking up sailing at age forty would turn into a lifelong passion. I never thought I would have tried to sail without instruments through a life-threatening storm in the

North Atlantic, learning what I did about sailing and my own character. I hadn't planned to get a master's, let alone a doctorate, when I had been an underachiever in high school. Even this book is a dream I wasn't sure would come true.

It's impossible to predict where your life will go—how the wind will change your course or who will be on the boat for the different legs of the journey. But we do have a choice, and that is to grab the helm of our lives and stand there firmly. Set aside the notion that the destination is more important than the journey—that once you achieve *that* goal or *this* success, that you have arrived, you are finished, you have won the game. There is no game to win, just your life to lead, and if you lead it with intention and gratitude and in the service of others, you will find your purpose, and once you find your purpose, meaning will not be far behind.

My hope for you is to strive for your purpose, to take ownership of your life. At the same time, have fun, embrace the joy and beauty of the world. This is also important for your well-being. I'm reminded of an E. B. White quotation: "I arise in the morning torn between a desire to improve the world and a desire to enjoy the world. This makes it hard to plan the day."

It's a beautiful quote, profound, even, but why make it one or the other? In fact, the point of Leading from the Helm is that if you do it right—that is, if you live life with passion, purpose, and intention, if you grab the helm—you can improve the world and enjoy it at the same time.

Like Janelle's advice to the young Rahim, stay in the now, take it one day at a time. Every once in a while—one week, one month, one year from now—go back to the reflections you wrote in this book or your notebook as you read. How have you grown? What are you discovering about yourself and your journey? Continue to stay open to the opportunities that arise, yet stay focused on your purpose, on serving your crew and leveraging your talents so that you are ready to step through the next door that opens to you. When the spokes of the helm are aligned with the way you live your life, you are on course to your true calling.

APPENDIX

OTHER RESOURCES

We at Sicora Consulting hope that you grab hold of your life passionately and full of confidence and knowledge. In addition to the Individual Helm and the Organizational Helm and the four color energies we discuss in the book, we offer a number of other tools that will help you gain the self-awareness that is so critical to Leading from the Helm. If you have questions about how these tools may work for you, please reach out to us in any of the ways listed on the last page.

Discover the Leader Within

Sicora Consulting was founded on the fundamental tenet that everyone has leadership within them. We develop leaders at all levels of an organization, helping executives and employees discover their individual strengths and unique leadership styles. Then we teach the organization to harness that collective power to unlock the higher level of performance every organization seeks.

8 Styles of Personality

The 8 Styles of Personality builds on the four color energies. Everyone has a unique combination of the eight personality styles that determines how they interact with others on an individual and team level. When we understand our preferences and those of the others we are engaging with, we gain the ability to adapt and connect our styles in a way that builds trust in relationships. In a group context, we learn to appreciate others' styles and differences and build a culture of diversity and inclusion. This creates greater value in relationships and greater value and benefit to the team and organization.

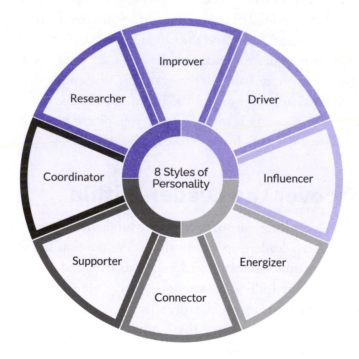

Purposeful Culture of Trust

Trust is the foundation of a healthy organization's culture. When leaders and team members engage in honest dialogue and act in a way that demonstrates integrity, relationships are solidified and business objectives are realized. This leads to a higher value for the customer.

In your organization, is there trust between leadership and employees? Does that trust span the organization from one team member to another? And do customers trust that you'll deliver on your promises? If there is any doubt in these questions, contact us today. Building trust is invaluable to the success of an organization.

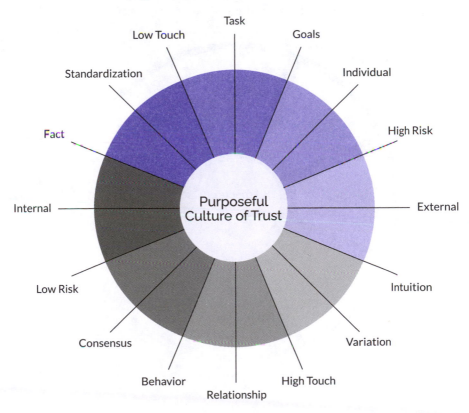

Team Effectiveness

Are your teams as productive as they could be? Are they balanced in their approach to how they serve each other and customers? To enhance team performance and to increase your organization's return on investment, it is important to analyze team effectiveness. Sicora Consulting uses a variety of methods to assess and elevate team performance. The 8 Aspects of a Balanced Team is one of them.

Trust is just one element that makes up an effective team. Multiple other factors in the model bring balance to the team and maximize the potential of both the individual and the team. When all these aspects work in concert, the team's performance is greatly amplified.

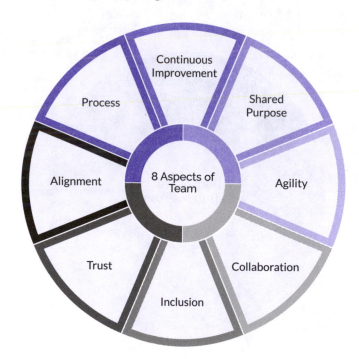

8 Factors of Engagement

Employee engagement is the leading indicator of success for any organization. This is why organizations that listen and respond to the needs of employees deliver better results. Sicora Consulting helps organizations move away from annual, event-based engagement models to an employee-led culture of continuous improvement. When employees remain engaged over a sustained period of time, superior results follow.

Highly engaged employees lead to increased productivity and greater customer satisfaction. Sicora Consulting knows how to drive the highest levels of employee engagement. To demonstrate the true impact, our tools measure the link between engagement and key business indicators. With Leading from the Helm and the 8 Factors of Engagement, we help you create an employee-led culture of continuous engagement that ensures the success of your business increases along with its engagement scores.

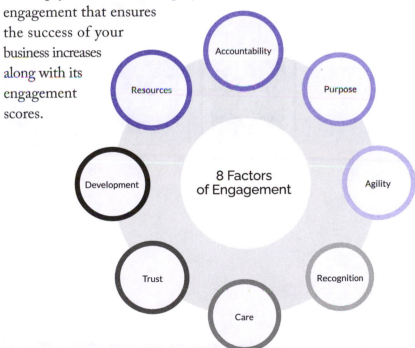

Organizational Impact Analysis

There are many benefits to our process linking employee engagement to organizational impact. First, that link demonstrates the return on investment of employee engagement and gains buy-in using the organization's unique impact metrics. Second, our process targets specific engagement factors that are most critical to the organization's performance to drive meaningful action planning. Finally, we use data insights to drive other talent initiatives, such as development programs, leadership competencies, and the organization's employee value proposition.

Whether you have established key performance indicators or have just a general sense of strategic goals, Sicora Consulting will help you uncover how employee engagement drives processes, customer experience, and the organization's bottom line.

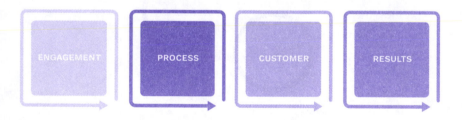

ACKNOWLEDGMENTS

Mary Pumper has worked with me from the beginning on the project that became this book, *Grab the Helm*, and I thank her for all the writing, rewriting, editing, and project management—well beyond the call of duty!

I'd like to thank the editor and writer Charles Grosel of Write for Success for helping us rework the manuscripts of earlier versions of *Grab the Helm*.

Many others have contributed to the development of Leading from the Helm, the program, and *Grab the Helm*, the book: David Williams, Barbara Hoese, Bob Thele, and the Crow Wing County Minnesota Leadership Team.

And of course, I am deeply indebted to my crew members at Sicora Consulting: Erin, Ian, Laura, Adam, Jason, and Val.

ABOUT THE AUTHOR

Dr. Robert T. Sicora, founder of Sicora Consulting and creator of Leading from the Helm, is a recognized organization development and human resources thought leader, consultant, facilitator, and speaker. He brings more than thirty years of experience in business and consulting to his practice and has helped thousands of employees and leaders rediscover themselves and their organization with his four main programs: Leading from the Helm, Discover the Leader Within, 8 Factors of Engagement, and Purposeful Culture of Trust.

With a background in strategic human resources, organization development, and process management, Dr. Sicora has successfully delivered results in multiple industries, including for-profit, nonprofit, academic, and government agencies, and small-, medium-, and large-growth companies.

Specializing in strategy, organizational culture, trust, employee engagement, leadership development, and team effectiveness, Dr. Sicora's aim is to provide every individual, team, organization, and community a holistic and unique perspective on how to transform themselves and grow to their full individual and collective potential.

Robert completed his doctorate of education (EdD) in organization development from the University of St. Thomas. He conducted research and wrote his dissertation on determining how personality styles of leaders and employees have an impact on the ability to create a culture of trust within organizations. He also holds a master's degree in human resource management from the Carlson School of Management at the University of Minnesota and undergraduate degrees in sociology and speech communications from St. Cloud State University, where he serves as President on the alumni board.

Robert is an avid sailor and adventurer and loves to travel. He lives in Minneapolis, Minnesota, USA.

Robert would love to stay in touch with you about your experience with the book in particular and the Leading from the Helm program in general. If you have any questions, aha moments, or stories to share, or are interested in supplemental resources, contact him in any of the following ways:

Email: DrRobTSicora@SicoraConsulting.com

Company Website: Sicoraconsulting.com

Book Website: GrabtheHelm.com

Firm's LinkedIn: linkedin.com/company/sicora-consulting-inc-

Robert's LinkedIn: https://www.linkedin.com/in/robertsicora

Facebook: facebook.com/SicoraConsulting

Twitter: @robtsicora

WORKS CITED

Leon Brown, https://www.passiton.com/inspirational-quotes/7971-never-underestimate-the-valuable-and-important, accessed July 1, 2020

Joseph Campbell, *The Power of Myth*, Anchor, 1991

Paulo Coelho, *Brida*, Harper Perennial, reprint edition, 2009

Roy E. Disney Quotes, BrainyQuote.com, BrainyMedia Inc, https://www.brainyquote.com/quotes/roy_e_disney_183365, accessed June 29, 2020

Benjamin Franklin, *Poor Richard's Almanack,* Peter Pauper Press, Large Edition, 1980

Viktor Frankl, *Man's Search for Meaning*, Beacon Press, 2014

Carl Jung, *C.G. Jung Society of New Orleans Newsletter*, Spring 2016, Col. 25, No.1

Joseph P. Lash, *Helen and Teacher: The Story of Helen Keller and Anne Sullivan Macy*, A Merloyd Lawrence Book, Delacorte Press/Seymour Lawrence, 1980

Richard Leider, https://richardleider.com/author-qa/

Nelson Mandela, *Long Walk to Freedom*, Back Bay Books, 2018

Eckhart Tolle, *The Power of* Now: *A Guide to Spiritual Enlightenment*, New World Library, 2004

E. B. White Quotes, BrainyQuote.com, BrainyMedia Inc., https://www.brainyquote.com/quotes/e_b_white_106410, accessed July 10, 2020